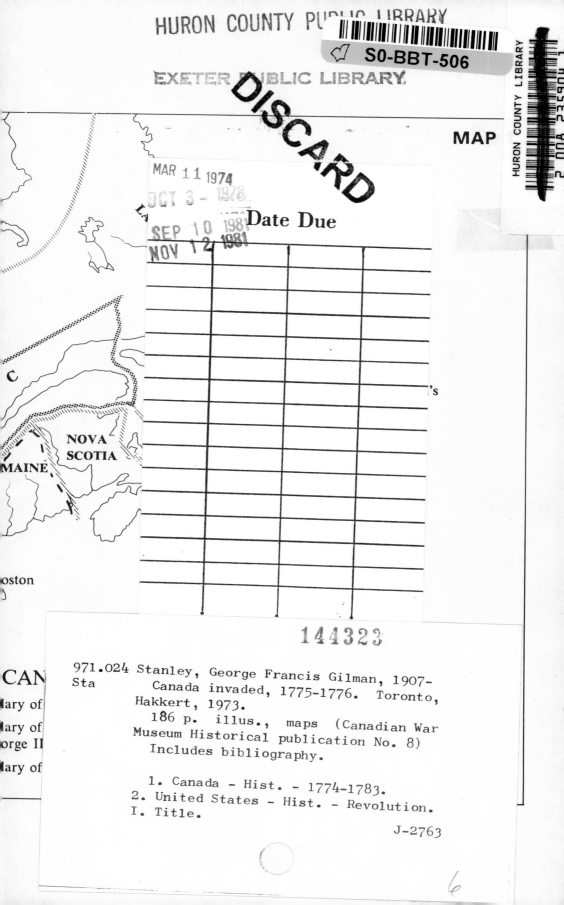

NOVA
SCOTIA

MAINE

C

oston

CAN

ary of

ary of

orge II

ary of

6

R. Marrion
71

Canadian War Museum

Historical Publications Number 8

Editor: John Swettenham
        Curator, Historical Resources

George F. G. Stanley

CANADA INVADED
1775-1776

HAKKERT   TORONTO   1973

Cover:
The Fight at the Sault-au-Matelot
From a colour drawing by C. W. Jefferys

Frontispiece:
Officer of the Royal Highland Emigrants
By R. Marrion

This book has been written and published
with the aid of funds provided by the
National Museums of Canada.

Standard Book Number: 88866-537-7
Library of Congress Catalogue Card
Number: 73-88116

A. M. Hakkert Ltd.,
554 Spadina Crescent
Toronto, Canada M5S 2J9

Printed in Canada by The Hunter Rose Co.

Previous publications in the series:

[1] *Canada and the First World War*, by
John Swettenham. Canadian War
Museum, Ottawa, 1968.

[2] *D-Day*, by John Swettenham.
Canadian War Museum, Ottawa, 1969.

[3] *Canada and the First World War*, by
John Swettenham. Based on the Fiftieth
Anniversary Armistice Display at the
Canadian War Museum. Ryerson,
Toronto, 1969. Illustrated.

[4] *Canadian Military Aircraft*, by J. A.
Griffin. Queen's Printer, Ottawa, 1969.

5 *The Last War Drum: the North West
Rebellion of 1885*, by Desmond Morton.
Published by Hakkert, Toronto, in
co-operation with the Canadian War
Museum, 1972.

6 *The Evening of Chivalry*, by John
Swettenham. National Museums of
Canada, Ottawa, 1972.

7 *Valiant Men: Canada's Victoria Cross
and George Cross Winners*, edited by
John Swettenham. Hakkert, Toronto,
1973.

To the Memory of My Great Great Grandfather
Matthew Wyn Stanley
of H.M. 24th Regiment of Foot,
who served in North America 1790-1802
and with the 1st Regiment, Stormont Militia
during the Canadian War of 1812

fois do t'anam

Foreword

Since 1967 the Canadian War Museum has been in much larger premises than formerly and our plan of presenting a complete review of Canada's military past, from the time of early exploration and settlement up to the recent unification of the armed forces, is well advanced. The displays, of which we already have a number, will consist of a brief storyline, graphics, and the most appropriate artefacts of our rather large collection.

There is just so much that one can say in a storyline. We seek also, therefore, to provide books and booklets for those who want more than can be given on the walls. And for that reason we are most grateful to historians who say, as George Stanley did, "I can assure you that I am willing to do what I can to further the cause of military history in this country."

In this book Dr. Stanley describes a crucial phase in Canadian history — the invasion of Canada by American forces in 1775, the "struggle for the fourteenth colony," and the repulse of the invaders at Quebec. Unfulfilled ambitions and the latent hostility which flared into war again in 1812 will be the subject of another of our studies.

George Stanley is too well known a military historian to require further introduction here. His work, in this book, speaks for itself and it remains only to say that we are proud of his association with our programme.

Lee F. Murray
Chief Curator,
Canadian War Museum.

Preface

During a visit to Mount Allison University in 1972, John Swettenham suggested to me that I might write an account of the American invasion of Canada in 1775 for publication by the Canadian War Museum in Ottawa. The suggestion appealed to me, if only because, some years previous while on a Guggenheim Fellowship, I had already done some of the research required to prepare such an account. It also seemed to me to be a timely subject in view of the approaching bicentenary of the American Revolutionary War, from which Canada emerged with contracted frontiers, but with her separate identity confirmed by force of arms and international agreement. The first effort to incorporate Canada into a continental union was defeated at Quebec. This book is an outline of how this was done.

For assistance in obtaining research materials, I acknowledge, with gratitude, my indebtedness to John W. Spurr, a former comrade-in-arms and now librarian at the Royal Military College of Canada, Miss Eleanor Magee, librarian at Mount Allison University, Dr. F. F. Thompson, R. P. Adrien Pouliot s.j., Jean-Jacques Lefebvre, Dr. James Maclean of Glensanda the Younger, Lieutenant Colonel R. Campbell Preston, Reverend D. A. L. Maclean of Dochgarroch, and Mrs. Maclean, Captain A. Farquharson of Invercauld and Torloisk, M.C., and Lieutenant Colonel George B. Dyer. For prints of the illustrations and permission to reproduce them, I am obliged to The Lord Maclean, K.T., G.C.V.O., K.B.E., to my personal friends, Mrs. John Nicholas Brown and Mr. Harrison K. Bird, and to the Public Archives of Canada, les Archives Nationales du Quebec, the National Gallery of Canada, the National Museum of Man, the U.S. National Gallery of Art, the Smithsonian Institution, the New York Public Library, the Historical Society of Pennsylvania, the Historical Society of Rhode Island, the Company of Military Historians, Yale University, Brown University, and Stackpole Books.

Miss Heather Hargrave typed the manuscript; Mr. E. H. Ellwand drew the maps; and Dr. Desmond Morton, a former student of mine and now Associate Professor of History at Erindale, placed the illustrations in the proper order when the text was being printed. To each of them I express my thanks. For the kind of encouragement and practical help that every author needs and appreciates, I have always relied upon my wife, Ruth.

St. Dunstan's Day 1973.

George F. G. Stanley,
Sackville, New Brunswick

Table of Contents

Picture Credits:

List of Illustrations and Maps

Maps

Sir Guy Carleton

I The Propaganda War 1774-1775

I. The Quebec Act

On September 18th, 1774, Guy Carleton landed at Quebec. After four years' absence from Canada, he was returning from London to resume his responsibilities as governor of the province of Quebec. With him he brought his wife, Lady Maria Howard, a woman less than half his age, whom he had met, wooed and married while in England, and their two children. He also brought a copy of a document known officially as an "Act for making more effectual Provision for the Government of the Province of Quebec." This Act, one of the most important state papers in the history of North America, had after long consideration by the members of the British government and rough treatment at the hands of the members of the British House of Commons, received the signature of George III on June 22nd.

It was 1770 when Carleton had left the Chateau of St. Louis, high on the cliff above the river at Quebec, to carry his advice on the political problems of Canada and their possible solutions directly to his superiors in London. By that time he had served two years as governor of the province, having succeeded to the appointment on the recall of James Murray, whose failure to implement the British assimilation policy had been so strongly resented by the Anglo-American merchants who had come to Montreal and Quebec following the British military victories of 1759 and 1760. With Murray out of the way, the English-speaking minority in the province had hoped for much from the new governor. But Carleton was no friend of the merchants, neither was he a friend of the politicians. His training, experience of the Seven Years' War and prejudices disposed him to see the Canadian problem as essentially a military one. He looked upon France as Great Britain's natural enemy, and to him it seemed the natural course of things to anticipate that France would make an effort to recover her lost dominions in North America. To minimize the dangers inherent in such a possibility was in Carleton's opinion the obvious course to follow. This might best be achieved by providing the king's new French Canadian subjects with employment in

3

the armed services and by conciliating their natural leaders, the noblesse and the clergy. Employment and conciliation might go far towards gaining goodwill and eliminating the possibility of French Canadian support of France in another Anglo-French war. Or, at least, so Carleton believed.[1]

Despite the strenuous efforts of the Anglo-American mercantile and Protestant elements in Canada to influence the British government by their petitions, and the representations of Francis Masères, their agent in London, it was Carleton's point of view that carried the greater weight. To the merchants' petitions, Carleton could oppose those of the French Canadian seigneurs, who, if they were truly representative of the people of the province (and who in London was to say they were not?) spoke for a population far more numerous than that of their rivals. Apparently what French Canadians really wanted was recognition of their language, religious and legal rights and "a share of the civil and military employments under His Majesty's Government."[2] Nothing more. The Anglo-Americans might talk repeatedly of the need to establish an elected "General Assembly" in Quebec, but the French Canadians said simply, in reply, that they desired "a council that should consist of a greater number of members than that which has hitherto subsisted in the province, and that should be composed partly of his majesty's old subjects, and partly of his new ones." Such a council, they argued, "would be a much fitter instrument of government" than a general assembly "for the province in its present state."[3]

The Quebec Act, in its final form, was definitely a bid for the support of the Canadian people and their leaders; it was also an act of political and economic justice. This was true of the rectification of the boundary which had been contracted and distorted by the Proclamation of 1763. By the terms of that document, Canada had been reduced to a narrow parallelogram, bisected by the St. Lawrence, and terminated on the east by Labrador and the Gaspé peninsula, and on the west by a line just south of the Ottawa River. Elsewhere, all that had been left to New France of French Acadia after the Treaty of Utrecht in 1713 had been included in Nova Scotia; the southern boundary had been moved north from the south end of Lake Champlain to the 45th parallel of latitude; and the region west and south of the Ottawa, extending to the Mississippi and including the Ohio, had been made into a vast Indian Territory beyond the jurisdiction of Canada or that of any of the American colonies. The Quebec Act, although it did nothing about the eastern or southern boundaries of the province, did at least extend the western frontier to embrace the former Indian Territory which had been tied geographically, economically, politically, and ethnically to Canada prior to the collapse of French rule in North America. This measure of the Quebec Act thus promised to bring law and order to a region given over to the miseries, licence and confusion of unregulated free trade, and restore strength to a Canadian economy ruined by war and constricted boundaries.

Even more reasonable, from the Canadian standpoint, were those clauses of the Quebec Act which gave sanction and definition to the civil law of Canada and the prevailing system of land tenure. English criminal law might be acceptable to French Canadians, but what had English civil law to contribute towards ironing out the problems of seigneurialism? As far as the administration of the province was concerned, the French Canadians received exactly what they had asked for, an enlarged council, nearly twice the size of the old one, comprising not less than seventeen members and not more than twenty-three. And, more significant still, French Canadians were to be eligible for appointment to this new body. The old oath, which made it impossible for a Roman Catholic to accept governmental office, was replaced in the Quebec Act by a new innocuous oath from which all the objectionable features had been removed. Not least important was the provision by the Quebec Act for full recognition of the right of the Roman Catholic church, not only to carry out its traditional services and rituals, but also to collect its tithes from the faithful, reserving to the crown the right to levy tithes upon the Protestant population for the support of the Protestant clergy should the need arise.

One cannot but recognize the reasonableness and fairness which motivated Carleton and the others who drafted this Act and forced it through Parliament, even if one is disposed to question their political foresightedness. In granting emancipation to Catholics in Canada over half a century before a similar measure of relief was given to their co-religionists in the United Kingdom, the parliament of Great Britain was acting well in advance of its time. But such religious liberality was a hard thing for many people of that day to digest. The prejudices of two hundred years, confirmed by the execution of one king and the expulsion of another, were not easily set aside, even by a generation which prided itself upon its rationalism and its broadmindedness. Sincere the opponents of the Quebec Act may have been, but sincerity all too frequently sharpens the cutting edge of bigotry. Nor was it easy to convince Englishmen that English laws and English legal procedures were not necessarily the unquestioned best that man could devise. Some of the liberty-loving exponents of a general assembly for Canada could see no conflict of principle and practice when they proposed to consign the lives and fortunes of one hundred thousand French Canadian Roman Catholics to the potential tyranny of a handful of alien, Protestant merchants.[4] Even the Corporation of the City of London saw nothing ironic in appealing to George III, as Defender of the Faith (a title conferred upon Henry VIII by Pope Leo X) to withhold his signature from a measure which its members professed to believe might establish popery in North America.

On his return to Canada, Carleton and his Versailles-educated wife were received with ceremony and with every mark of respect on the part of the French Canadian gentry. The noblesse and clergy were loud in their praises of the Quebec Act, and no less than fifty Canadian seigneurs hurried from Montreal to pay homage to the governor and the Lady Maria and to enjoy the hospitality of the Chateau of St. Louis in Quebec. Whatever the criticisms may have been in Great Britain, Carleton felt that he had reason to believe that the Act which he had sponsored responded to the needs and the demands of the Canadian situation and of the Canadian people. He therefore took the first opportunity of writing to the Earl of Dartmouth, one of the King's principal Secretaries of State, to report that he had found "His Majesty's Canadian Subjects impressed with the strongest sense of The King's great Goodness towards them" and that "All Ranks of People amongst them vied with each other in testifying their Gratitude and Respect, and the Desire they have by every Mark of Duty and Submission to prove themselves not undeserving of the Treatment they have met with."[5] The governor may have been gilding the truth somewhat, but he was not violating any of his own convictions.

One thing, however, had been missing from Carleton's dispatch, and Dartmouth had been quick to note it. That was the absence of any reference to the attitude of the English-speaking minority towards the Quebec Act. In his reply to Carleton, he drily observed that, "As you are silent as to the Sentiments of His Majesty's Natural born Subjects in Canada respecting the late Act, I am not at liberty to conclude that they entertain the same opinion of it" as the Canadians. Such being the case then it would be Carleton's responsibility to "persuade" them "of the justice and propriety of the present form of Government and of the attention that has been shewn to their Interests not only in the adoption of the English laws, as far as it was consistent with what was due to the just Claims and moderate Wishes of the Canadians, but in the opening to the British Merchant, by an Extension of the Province, so many new Channels of important Commerce."[6] If they could not satisfy their political ambitions, the English-speaking merchants might, at least, be able to satisfy their financial aspirations. In imposing this task upon the governor of Canada, Dartmouth was, whether he knew it or not, asking Carleton to do the impossible.

The king's natural-born subjects, the Anglo-American minority in Montreal and Quebec, emphatically did not like the Quebec Act. By accepting the aristocratic principle of an appointed council, the Act thwarted their ambitions to gain political power through an elected council; by its concessions to the Roman Catholic church, the Act offended their sensibilities as Protestants; by failing to impose trial by jury the Act deprived them of the Englishman's traditional privilege of submitting his civil suits to the decision of twelve ignorant jurors instead of one learned judge. All the Act left them was an opportunity to expand their commercial interests in the old western areas of the province. The Act, in a few words, was the embodiment of everything they had opposed since the days of General Murray, and the denial of everything for which they had agitated since they had drawn up their first petition for an assembly and hired a lobbyist to press their case in London in 1765.

Lady Carleton

The merchants' quarrel with Murray and Carleton was not based upon the principles of political democracy. Rather was it a conflict between a new, rising, urban, middle class, deriving its strength from its exploitation of the colony's economic resources[7] and a declining, landed aristocracy deriving its strength from its military service and its social pretensions. The merchants saw their hopes for power in the control of an elected assembly, and the governing elite relied for its retention of power upon its control of patronage and the militia. To add to the confusion as well as the bitterness of this politico-social contest, there was the religious factor, the rivalry of Roman Catholicism and Protestantism, the former finding its principal support among the aristocratic and governmental elite, and the latter drawing its strength from the bourgeoisie. Neither group saw any virtue in the other, while each saw itself as the true representative of the national interest.

There had been no love lost between them ever since that day in December 1764, when several men with blackened faces burst into the house of Thomas Walker, one of the leading members of the English merchant community, beat him severely and cut off his ear. Walker, a large, beardless, raw-red faced man who had come to Montreal from Boston in 1763, had made himself particularly objectionable to an arrogant young officer of the 28th Regiment, and it was suspected that the assailants belonged to that particular corps. Several arrests were made, but, owing to lack of evidence, the charges were dismissed. Walker was convinced that he could obtain no justice from the magistrates, and his fellow merchants seethed with resentment against Governor Murray and spared no efforts to bring about the governor's recall. It did not help relations between the merchants and the administration when, shortly after the arrival of Guy Carleton, John McCord

Thomas Walker, the Anglo-American merchant who acted as the principal agent of Congress in Montreal, and who collaborated with the invaders in 1775.

set up several liquor outlets near the military barracks in Quebec. McCord's establishments were promptly placed out of bounds to the troops, whereupon the owner, according to Carleton, finding himself deprived of a lucrative trade, promptly "commenced Patriot, and with the Assistance of . . . three or four more, egged on by Letters from Home," renewed their demands for a popular assembly. Carleton had no use for elected bodies as tending to encourage the spread of "Republican Principles," and inquired of his superiors whether "the independent Spirit of a Democracy is well adapted to a subordinate Government of the British Monarchy," and whether such "uncontrolable Notions" should be tolerated "in a Province, so lately Conquered and Circumstanced as this is."[8]

In October 1773, when the preparations for the Quebec Bill were already far advanced, the merchants of the town of Quebec formed a committee, under the chairmanship of McCord, to draft representations to be sent to London. McCord made an effort to enlist the support of some of the more influential French Canadians, but found them unwilling to become involved in measures which were of more concern to the English community than to the French. He found, however, no difficulty in getting help from Thomas Walker, who rushed off from Montreal to Quebec to encourage the agitation in the provincial capital. With Walker's help, McCord, Zachary Macaulay, and several other Quebec merchants drafted a petition to be sent to London. This achieved, Walker then returned to Montreal where, with his friends, he drew up a document similar to that which he had helped prepare at Quebec. The Montreal petition, in addition to the signatures of Walker and his nephew, carried, among others, those of James McGill, James Price, Joseph Bindon and William Haywood. Both petitions were then forwarded to Masères, who passed them on to the Earl of Dartmouth. To advise Masères and to solicit support from the business community of London, Walker and Macaulay spent part of the winter in England.

In spite of Walker's activity it must have been clear to most of the Anglo-American merchants in Canada that little was really to be hoped for from the petitions and representations they had been induced to make. Official opinion in England was running too strongly against them. Even if they did gain support from their mercantile colleagues in London and from the corporation of England's principal city, they could not induce the ministers of the Crown to listen more intently to the skilful arguments of Francis Masères than to the less accomplished explanations of Guy Carleton, and the impugned Act for the more effective government of Quebec went through its various readings to become law in the summer of 1774. Even then, however, the more stubborn merchants refused to admit defeat. Scarcely more than a fortnight after Carleton's triumphal return to Quebec, the indefatigable Walker was hard at work raising money and drumming up support for another petition. Early in October he went to Quebec and called an open meeting of the English-speaking inhabitants of the town. Several such gatherings were held, according to Carleton,[9] at which resolutions were adopted expressing thanks for the assistance afforded by the Lord Mayor and Corporation of London, offering a substantial inducement to Masères to continue his work as London agent, and proposing the despatch of three more petitions to Great Britain. Carleton was well informed of Walker's efforts to ignite the spirit of disaffection − "nocturnal Cabals" he called Walker's meetings − but raised no hand to stay him. It seemed enough simply to keep Dartmouth informed of what was going on in Canada. The earl would learn soon enough. Within days of receiving Carleton's report, Masères was handing him the three petitions recently arrived from Canada, one addressed to the Crown, one to the House of Lords, and one to the House of Commons. Dartmouth saw that they carried no less than 186 signatures, a substantial proportion of the total male English-language population of the country, if we accept Carleton's estimate of their numbers, 360, as reasonably accurate.[10]

It is doubtful if many of those who penned their names to the three petitions, except perhaps the more fanatical among them, really expected that the British government would completely reverse its policy and repeal an Act which it had adopted only six months previously. Perhaps the sponsors of the petitions thought the threatening developments in the Thirteen Colonies might induce the ministers to take another look at the Quebec Act. But this is only surmise. It was equally likely that the defiant actions of the American colonists would harden rather than weaken the ministers' attitude. In any event, instead of repealing the Quebec Act the government merely confirmed its previous decision, and on June 7th, 1775, Dartmouth informed the governor of Canada of how little impression the Opposition's attack on the Act had made. "To all appearance," he wrote, "the People of England, in general, concur in the Measures which have been adopted for America."[11] Three weeks later he was writing again to Carleton, this time with considerably less complacency, urging the governor to take immediate steps to raise a military force of 3000 Canadians as a precaution against any spread of the American rebellion.

The winter and spring months which followed Carleton's return to Quebec on September 18th, 1774, were months of gradual disillusionment for the governor of Canada. He had come back to Canada full of confidence in the virtues of his Act and hopes for his own future. Impressed by the French Canadian expressions of satisfaction with what he had brought from London by way of a new constitution, Carleton promptly responded to a request received on the 19th from the commander in chief of the British forces in North America, General Thomas Gage, for the immediate despatch to Boston of two regiments of British regulars from the Canadian garrison, the 10th and the 52nd. Since this would leave Carleton with only two under-strength regiments, the 7th and 26th, to maintain order in a country and peace on a frontier which was shortly to be expanded to include the Ohio Valley, Gage had asked him whether, "should matters come to Extremities," a "Body of Canadians and Indians might be collected, and confided in, for Service in this Country."[12] In a state of euphoric trust, Carleton replied, "The Canadians have testified to me the strongest marks of Joy, and Gratitude, and Fidelity to the King, and to His Government, for the late Arrangements made at Home in their Favour; a Canadian Regiment would compleat their happiness, which in Time of Need might be augmented to two, three or more Battalions, tho' for the Satisfaction of the Province, and 'till the Kings Service might require more, one would be sufficient. . . ." As far as the Indians were concerned, he believed them to be "in very good Humour," although — and here he sounded a muted note of warning — "you know what sort of People they are."[13]

As the weeks went by, the bright hopes of the autumn faded and Carleton's euphrasy passed. In November he was beginning to worry about the activities of Walker and his associates and the unsettling effect their agitations were having upon the French Canadian population. He was obviously uneasy about the sheaves of political propaganda from the Thirteen Colonies circulating out of Montreal into the rural constituencies with the help of Anglo-American malcontents with trading correspondents along the St. Lawrence and Richelieu rivers. When he wrote to Gage on February 4th, 1775, he was considerably less sanguine about the prospects of raising a military force among the local population. It was not that he was

John McCord, one of the leaders of the opposition to the Quebec Act and an opponent of Guy Carleton.

concerned about the willingness of the noblesse to enter military service, rather was he apprehensive of the lack of enthusiasm on the part of the habitants who, he confessed, "have in a manner emancipated themselves" and would require time "and discreet management" to be recalled "to their ancient habits of obedience and discipline." There was a note of gloomy truth in his subsequent remark, "Considering all the new ideas they have been acquiring for these ten years past, can it be thought they will be pleased at being suddenly and without preparation embodied into a militia and marched from their families, lands, and habitations to remote provinces and all the horrors of war which they have already experienced. It would give an appearance of truth to the language of our sons of sedition, at this very moment busily employed instilling into their minds that the Act was passed merely to serve the present purposes of Government and in the full intention of ruling over them with all the despotism of their ancient masters."[14]

If Carleton had reason to harbour doubts about the depth of French Canadian professions of fidelity and willingness to serve the king, he had even more reason to doubt the sincerity of the loyalty of the English-speaking population concentrated in the two strategic centres of the country, Quebec and Montreal. To judge from their actions during the winter of 1774–1775 — about which he was reasonably well informed — they were not a group upon whom he could rely. All he could hope for would be a recognition of the futility of continued opposition to the new constitution and a reasonable attempt to make it work.

The day set for the inauguration of the new constitution was May 1st. On the morning of that day the citizens of Montreal were astonished and dismayed to find the bust of the king, George III, which stood in one of the public places in Montreal, daubed with black paint, while suspended around the royal neck had been placed a rosary made of potatoes with a wooden cross bearing the words, "Voilà le Pape du Canada et le Sot Anglois."

The authorities and the loyal citizens were furious. The military blamed the merchants and their seditious committees — who else would so dare to insult the king? The French Canadian Roman Catholics blamed the English Protestants — who else would thus insult Christ's holy church and make so clumsy an attempt to throw suspicion upon the French population? Some people thought it had been done by the Jews; others were convinced that it was the work of Yankee malcontents. A certain Sieur LePailleur's outspoken suspicions involved him in a fistic altercation with a Jew, Ezekial Salomons, and the Sieur Francois Marie Picoté de Belestre was driven to an exchange of blows with an American by the name of Franks. A military guard paraded the streets, and Governor Carleton issued a proclamation promising to reward any informer with two hundred piastres, if he would furnish the necessary evidence which would lead to the arrest and conviction of the culprit or culprits. Franks was hustled off to prison by the military guard, but when no evidence could be brought against him, he was released on Carleton's orders, a sadder and a more bellicose man. No one could be persuaded — or had the temerity — to come forward to claim the government's two hundred piastres; and the bitterness engendered by the disfigurement of the king's bust did not soon pass away. It was an act as stupid in its conception as it was provocative in its results. It served no other purpose than to exacerbate feelings already raw from the friction of repeated charges and counter-charges — although it is not beyond the bounds of possibility that that was, indeed, the original motive behind it.

II. The Thirteen Colonies and the Quebec Act

More outspoken and more virulent by far in their criticism of the Quebec Act than either the British opponents of the Act or the Anglo-American merchants of Montreal and Quebec, were the American inhabitants of the Thirteen Colonies. They had, in fact, been complaining about the British government and its actions ever since the victories of Amherst's armies in Canada had removed the French threat to their own frontiers. As early as 1764, the American trader and Indian agent, George Croghan, had written to Sir William Johnson from London, "Nothing has been Don respecting North America. . . There has been Nothing Don Sence I came to London by the Grate ones butt Squebeling & fighting (to) See who will keep in power."[15]

But disgust with the intrigue and jobbery of British eighteenth century politics was not the main cause of the antagonism that developed between the British and colonial administrations. It was the important financial issue of whether or not the Americans, in whose interests many people in Great Britain felt the Seven Years' War had been fought, were going to help defray the costs of that war. By 1763 Great Britain was financially exhausted and the bulk of the British troops were still stationed in the colonies. The British politicians, faced with the dual problems of meeting a high defence budget and the unemployment that seems so frequently to follow the cessation of ephemeral wartime demands, not unnaturally looked to the colonies for relief. To the British mind it seemed only fair that the Americans should make some contribution towards the mounting costs of imperial defence, and only natural, too, that the British Parliament should exercise its right to determine how much this contribution should be and how it should be collected.

Even in the colonies there were some who believed that the British contention was not unreasonable; what they found unpalatable was the insistence by British ministers on the right of Parliament to impose financial burdens upon the people of the colonies without obtaining their prior consent. To allow Great Britain to impose taxes in this way struck at the very heart of the American colonists' nascent nationalism and the growing sense of their own self-importance. In this way a straightforward financial matter, which might otherwise have been settled satisfactorily and amicably at the executive level, was dragged into the charged atmosphere of party politics and became a stalking horse for contentious issues which were the outcome, on the one hand of ministerial pedantry, and on the other, of a heady sense of freedom born of release from the traditional fear of incursions across their frontiers from Canada.

Perhaps the explanation of the blunders which seemed to come so readily from the ministerial offices in Great Britain in these post-1763 years, is to be found in the failure of the British to realize that their colonies had, in fact, never really been theirs; the colonists might, when it suited their purposes, claim the rights of Englishmen, but the American colonies had not really been founded as extensions of England and of the English way of life in North America. Rather, they existed as rejections of that particular way of life. Those men who had established the original settlements along the Atlantic seaboard had done so with the deliberate object of escaping from the restrictions which England had imposed upon them; restrictions, religious, political and social which had become intolerable. The descendants of the settlers who had turned their backs on the England they disliked could hardly be expected to look favourably upon taxes and duties imposed upon them by a government in London, or to welcome — except in times of war — the officers and men of the British regiments, the scarlet-coated "bloodybacks," who represented the most authoritarian aspect of the

English society their forefathers had abandoned.

In the absence of any sign of readiness on the part of the colonial legislatures to make some kind of a voluntary contribution to imperial defence, the British Parliament took several fatal steps, the first of which were the imposition of a stamp tax and the more rigorous enforcement of the Acts of Trade, particularly the molasses and sugar duties. Such measures led to protests and outcries from those classes of society most affected by them, the professional and business communities, both of which dominated the political scene in the several colonies.

The force of the American protests was such that the British government promptly repealed the Stamp Act. This action was politic in itself but it was rendered ineffective by the prompt imposition of a series of new duties upon various commodities in daily household use throughout the colonies, one of which was tea. With their minds still fixed on the costs of imperial defence, the British ministers failed to appreciate the strength of the hostility their insistence upon exercising their taxing powers was evoking in North America. Neither did they realize just how weak their position had become. Having given way to vigorous protest in one instance, could they expect the colonists quietly to acquiesce in the new imperial financial impositions? Opposition in America to the new duties was loud and instantaneous. There were indignant appeals to principle: "No taxation without representation." There were also overt appeals to force, and widespread rioting took place in Massachusetts. The British replied by sending additional troops to the port of Boston. The abrasive relationship which already existed between the British soldiery and the American populace was in no way reduced by the order given to the troops not to use their muskets or even to carry them loaded. Such orders only encouraged the aggressive elements in the community, and frequent efforts were made to provoke the soldiers into harsh action or induce them to desert. Then on March 5th, 1770, the Boston mob, emboldened by what they misinterpreted as cowardice, attacked the guard at the Customs' House; the troops were forced to use their weapons and to spill blood on the Boston streets. It was a miserable affair, this shooting at the Customs' House, although it was no abuse of power; but to demagogues like Samuel Adams "the maltster," it was a godsend. It could be, and was, dressed up in exaggerated terms as the "Boston Massacre" and paraded from one political platform to another.

The British ministers again drew in their horns. Almost anything should be conceded for the sake of peace, almost anything that is, except principle. Repealing the objectionable duties, the government clung stubbornly to the traditional doctrine of the supremacy of the imperial Parliament and its right to tax colonists abroad. For this reason it retained a token tax on tea. It is hard to explain such political ineptness except on the grounds of stubbornness; the tax on tea brought in little in the way of revenue and only nullified the appeasing effect the removal of the other duties might have had.

THE BLOODY MASSACRE PERPETRATED IN KING STREET, BOSTON, ON
MARCH 5TH, 1770, BY A PARTY OF THE 29TH REGIMENT.

The so-called "Boston Massacre" of March 5, 1770, as engraved, printed and sold by Paul
Revere. It was an effective "atrocity" document.

The closing of the port of Boston in retaliation for the dumping of the tea
cargoes of three East Indiamen into the harbour waters only served still
further to exacerbate American opinion, and the drinking of tea, hitherto a
pleasant and popular pastime carried over from old to New England, now
became a symbol of disloyalty. Committees were appointed in Boston to
inspect the premises of every tradesman to discourage him from selling the
offending beverage or of buying anything imported from Great Britain.

Some of those who attempted to defy the radicals were, according to an English traveller, tarred and feathered, while others had their property burned or destroyed by the populace. The centre of colonial militancy was the colony of Massachusetts, and particularly the town of Boston. But Boston was not alone in its posture of defiance. There was strong support forthcoming from New York and Charleston, and expressions of sympathy and gifts of wheat and money from as far away as Montreal and Quebec.

It was through the dark and distorted lenses of a growing hostility towards Great Britain that the American colonists viewed the Quebec Act with which Guy Carleton had been so very pleased. They resented it even more deeply than any of the previous "Intolerable Acts," if only because they had already embarked on the road which would lead them to rebellion and complete independence. To Alexander Hamilton, the refusal of Great Britain to grant elective, popular institutions to Canada as the Anglo-American merchants had demanded, was a signpost pointing towards a policy involving "the subjugation of the colonies, and afterward that of Great Britain itself."[16] The Quebec Act would surround the Protestant Colonies with "a Nation of Papists and Slaves." Obviously, he declared, "a superstitious bigotted Canadian Papist, though ever so profligate, is now esteemed a better subject to our Gracious Sovereign George the Third, than a liberal, enlightened New England Dissenter, though ever so virtuous."[17] Josiah Quincy professed to know that the British had made a secret treaty to establish Catholicism in Canada and restore that country to France and he conjured up all the old American bogeys: Frontenac, French and Canadian raids, shootings, knifings and scalpings. Others were even more terrified and terrifying with their talk of the Inquisition and "the carnage of a St. Bartholomew's Day" in Philadelphia. Others demanded belligerently to know why British ministers should cosset and suborn a people against whom Englishmen and Americans had been fighting for their lives for generations. To the extreme Protestants the religious provisions of the Quebec Act were positively wicked, the work of the Devil himself. The Act, they said, "must have caused a jubilee in Hell."[18]

It is hard to believe that the men who so misrepresented the intentions and terms of the Quebec Act and who appealed to the narrowest prejudices and to the blindest bigotry, really believed what they were saying. Today, their fears of subjugation, slavery, and popery, seem remote and meaningless. Were these men only sharpening their words to drive them deep beneath the skin, or were they simply uttering "loose sentences used for political ends"?[19] Perhaps. After all, demagoguery is not the prerogative of any one generation.

The clauses of the Quebec Act dealing with the liberties of the Roman Catholic church and the establishment of an enlarged council containing French Canadian members were those which made the greatest impact and which evoked the most intense feeling in Puritan, nonconformist, democratic

New England. Elsewhere, in New York, Pennsylvania and Virginia, the provisions which aroused the greatest resentment were those restoring to Canada the old western boundaries of New France. New York, Pennsylvania and Virginia, all had been interested in western expansion during the 1740s and 1750s, partly for purposes of trade, but even more significantly for the acquisition of land for purposes of settlement. The effort of Thomas Lee's Ohio Company to gain a foothold in the French dominions in the Ohio valley had been a major factor in prompting Virginia to send George Washington on the expedition which ended disastrously at Fort Necessity, and in rousing Great Britain to back the colonists by sending Braddock on his even more disastrous expedition to Fort Duquesne. For the British government now to restore to Canada the territory from which the French and Canadians had been expelled at the expense of American (and British) blood, seemed to argue the validity of the original pretentions of Louis XV and Governor Duquesne and to deny the justice of the American contentions of 1754. What was even more galling was the fact that the Canadian authorities would, in all likelihood, put a stop to any further American speculation in western lands for settlement purposes. And where would that leave men like George Washington, Patrick Henry and other speculators who had invested heavily in the Ohio region?

Thus several motives brought Americans from the various colonies together in common opposition to the policies of Great Britain as expressed in the Quebec Act. New England might see little advantage in forwarding the expansionist ambitions of her colonial neighbours — after all New England's outpost was Nova Scotia, a region in which the Virginian, George Washington, never showed much interest — but she could see an advantage in uniting her forces with those of the other colonies against the common enemies, Great Britain and the Quebec Act. Thus an act of parliament, intended basically to do justice to the French Canadians in sanctioning their natural right to enjoy their own laws and their own religion, was denounced by American patriots as being designed to do injustice to them by preventing the spread of American settlement and American liberties over the whole of the American continent. "The finger of God," said the *New York Journal or General Advertiser* on 20 July, 1775, "points out a mighty Empire to your sons; the Savages of the wilderness were never expelled to make room in this, the best part of the Continent, for idolators and slaves."

The news of the British parliament's adoption of the Quebec Act reached America just a fortnight before Carleton's return to Canada. Meanwhile the Thirteen Colonies had agreed to co-ordinate their protests against British policy, particularly after they had learned from their press what the terms of the Quebec Act actually were, and arrangements were concluded for a meeting of representatives of all the Colonies at Philadelphia on September 5th. The American people, as a whole, were not ready for an open break with Great Britain, and the Philadelphia Congress was bound to contain a great variety of political opinion; but the opportunity to press their views with vigour and determination in a forum such as the Congress would provide was not one the more radical elements were prepared to forego. Rich and poor, patrician and yeoman alike, once gathered at Philadelphia, proceeded to draft a Declaration of Rights, to renounce the drinking of tea, madeira and port (all of which were imported through England) and to denounce the coercive policy of the king's ministers. Aware of the agitation conducted by the mercantile minority of Quebec and Montreal against the Quebec Act, and aware, too, of the advantages of enlisting support in the St. Lawrence Valley, the members of the Continental Congress resolved to make their organization continental in fact as well as in name, and on October 26th addressed a long-winded homily to the people of Canada.

After trotting out the Marquis de Baccaria and "the immortal" Montesquieu to support their views, the American who drafted the Congress letter urged the people of Canada to "seize the opportunity presented . . . by Providence" to win freedom and gain representative government, by entering into a union with the other colonies, and to "take a noble chance for emerging from a humiliating subjection under Governors, Intendants, and Military Tyrants, into the firm rank and condition of free English citizens. . . ." The letter continued, "We are too well acquainted with the liberality of sentiment distinguishing your nation, to imagine, that difference of religion will prejudice you against a hearty amity with us. You know, that the transcendant nature of freedom elevates those, who unite in her cause, above all such low-minded infirmities. . . . It has been the universal pleasure and an unanimous vote, resolved, That we should consider the violation of your rights, by the Act for altering the government of your province, as a violation of our own, and that you should be invited to accede to our confederation, which has no other objects than the perfect security of the natural and civil rights of all the constituent members. . . ." Soft and high-minded as these words might at first sight appear, there was a big stick enclosed in the letter, a reminder to Canadians that it might be dangerous to reject the liberal invitation of Congress: "You are a small people, compared to those who with open arms invite you into a fellowship. A moment's reflection should convince you which will be most for your interest and happiness, to have all the rest of North America your unalterable friends, or your inveterate enemies."[20]

The Congress letter was translated and copies in both French and English were sent to Thomas Walker, that "great republican" whose pro-American proclivities had never been concealed, even from Carleton. The letter was also sent to the various newspapers in the colonies, and to the *Quebec Gazette* which refused to publish it. The *Gazette* was too dependent for its existence upon the continuance of government printing contracts to risk printing what was, by its very nature, a subversive document. Before the printed copies arrived in Montreal, the original letter had reached Walker, who promptly assembled the English-speaking merchants in the Coffee House and informed them of its contents. Plans were made at once to get in touch with the merchants in Quebec, and a committee, including Walker, was appointed for that purpose. Along the road to Quebec various agents distributed the printed copies, leaving them prominently displayed in public places and passing them from hand to hand. Carleton was not, apparently, prepared to take the matter very seriously, but, if we may judge from Jean Baptiste Badeaux's journal, the political propaganda from Congress was more widely and seriously read in the French regions of the province than the authorities suspected.[21] The noblesse and the clergy had welcomed the Quebec Act, but the average French Canadian had reserved judgement on it. He had no greater affection for tithes or feudal obligations than the American had for taxes, and all this talk of liberty from over the frontier was pretty warming stuff.

The Continental Congress was not the only American body interested in influencing public opinion in Canada in favour of the rebellious attitude adopted by the radicals in Massachusetts and elsewhere. A Committee of Correspondence had been formed in Boston with the object of entering into written communication with the other colonies, including Quebec. This committee consisted of Samuel Adams, John Hancock, Joseph Warren, Benjamin Church and John Brown, the last a young lawyer, resourceful and ambitious, who enjoyed the thrill of dabbling in politics, playing at soldiering and doing a little spying. Hearing that the Massachusetts Provincial Congress had been giving consideration to sending an agent to Canada, Brown wrote to Adams offering his services. He could, he promised, find out the truth of what was happening in Canada and provide Congress with the kind of intelligence it really needed. "Should you think proper to send me to execute this Business," he wrote, "I shall exert myself to the utmost of my Power in putting your orders into execution. Letters of recommendation will be necessary from you — expedition in prosecuting this most important Business is necessary and I will furnish you with a return before the next Session of Congress."[22] Brown's offer was accepted and, armed with letters from the Massachusetts Provincial Congress, from Samuel Adams and Joseph Warren, he set out for Albany and Montreal with two companions.

The journey was, as he had anticipated, a difficult one, replete with perils and hardship. It was, therefore, not until early April that he succeeded in reaching his destination. He immediately put himself in touch with Thomas Walker and spoke at a meeting of English-speaking inhabitants in the Coffee House. Despite his eloquence and his arguments, he found himself unable to persuade the Montreal merchants to go along with his proposal that they elect delegates to go to Philadelphia for the next sitting of the Continental Congress, even though he had the vocal support of Thomas Walker, James Price and Isaac Todd. All that he managed to obtain from them was a plaintive letter signed by Walker, Price, Haywood and John Wells deploring "the Sorrows and Afflictions, of our suffering Brethren" in Massachusetts, and offering their condolences and their good will. Nothing more. The time was not ripe, the English merchants contended, for more positive action; it would be impossible to send delegates to Congress, "which were we to attempt, the Canadians would join the Government to Frustrate." The real explanation was, of course, as Brown pointed out on his return, the fact that the policy adopted by Congress of prohibiting the importation of British goods would place the merchants of Montreal and Quebec at a serious disadvantage should the French Canadians refuse to go along with them. In these circumstances, the English would find themselves out in the cold while "the French would immediately monopolize the Indian Trade."[23] It was not that they were unsympathetic to "the Cause." They were. At least to the extent of asking the Americans how they might be of service to the opponents of the ministerial policy "without bringing down ruin upon our own heads." Unless Congress was willing to modify its economic policy, it was unlikely that it would ever obtain the whole-hearted support of the mercantile community in Canada, wherever the political sympathies of that group might lie.

Brown had not achieved what he set out to do when he embarked on his journey to Montreal. But his efforts were not a complete loss as far as the Americans were concerned. He had kept his eyes and his ears open, and he had carefully noted the weak state of the British garrisons at Ticonderoga, Crown Point and St. Jean. He also shrewdly concluded that the French Canadian habitants were not really as hostile to American ideas as the Montreal merchants feared they might be, and as Carleton was beginning to suspect they might not be.

The pace of events moved rapidly in the spring of 1775. On April 19th American militiamen clashed at Lexington with a detachment of British troops while resisting an attempt on the part of the latter to seize an illegal stockpile of warlike stores at Concord. To propagandists of the skill and style of Samuel Adams, the British actions on the 18th and 19th were grist to the political mill. The facts, with suitable embellishments, could be distorted enough to stir up the most belligerent feelings on the part of the people of Massachusetts. What was no more than a police action was blown up into a wanton, unprovoked attack upon women and children and helpless old men. Just about every atrocity story in the book was passed from mouth to ear, until the unfortunate bloodybacks of General Gage's army became the most hated people in the colony. It is questionable whether, after Lexington, it would have been possible for men to have sat down and discussed the whole unfortunate episode calmly and dispassionately; once passion entered the door, reason flew out the window, and both sides looked more to the priming of their muskets than to the tenets of their religion.

Ethan Allen's capture of Fort Ticonderoga on May 10, 1775.

III. The Capture of Ticonderoga

The immediacy of what was happening south of the frontier was brought home to the people and government of Canada several weeks later. On his way to Montreal, John Brown had taken a good look at Ticonderoga and had written to Samuel Adams that he believed the fort "must be seised as soon as possible should hostilities be committed by the King's Troops."[24] He suggested that the operation could probably best be carried out by a group of semi-outlaws living in the Hampshire grants and led by the Allen family, known as the "Bennington Mob" or "The Green Mountain Boys." These people had been annoying the administration and terrorizing the inhabitants of the northern part of New York for some years. They were rough, roistering, devil-may-care men, not particularly amenable to discipline, but capable of carrying out just such an operation as Brown suggested. Ethan Allen, their self-appointed commander, was ready and willing to do the job. He had been "electrified," he said,[25] by the news of Lexington, and had decided to submerge his dispute with New York in the larger struggle against the British; and how better to strike a blow for liberty than by taking possession of the great bogey fortress on Lake Champlain, whose name and reputation had always exceeded its real military potential? When his brother, Heman Allen, informed him that the colony of Connecticut would look favourably upon any effort to expel the British from the fort and was prepared to help in the task, Ethan Allen saw no reason for further hesitation.

Meanwhile another man of similar kidney had got hold of the idea of taking Ticonderoga. This was the ambitious, quick-witted, Benedict Arnold, who, after hearing of the repulse of the British troops at Lexington, had recruited a few men and rushed to Cambridge, Massachusetts, to offer his services to the "patriots." Here he persuaded the Provincial Congress to give him a commission as colonel, authorize him to raise a force of 500 men, supply him with funds and empower him to lead an attack upon the British position on Lake Champlain. Then, leaving the task of recruiting his force to his subordinate officers, he hurried off to the scene of what he expected would be his triumph. At Castleton he caught up with the bulk of Allen's force, produced his commission and prepared to take over command. The Green Mountain Boys would, however, have none of him. When Allen and Arnold met, the two men, so much alike and yet so different — both were resolute, egotistical swaggerers, although Allen possessed the generosity that Arnold never had, and Arnold the flair and aptitude for military operations that Allen believed he had but did not — found each other intolerable. Neither would yield to the other the leadership which each thought was peculiarly his own, and neither could be intimidated by the other. Allen had the men and Arnold had the commission, and in unbrotherly love they marched together at the head of the stumbling files of ill-uniformed men who captured Ticonderoga on May 10th, 1775. In Allen's *Narrative*, Arnold's name is never mentioned in the operation. It was Allen's show entirely.

The crossing of the lake was carried out under cover of darkness and at dawn on the 10th some eighty-three men climbed the ramparts and approached the iron-studded gate. Never a man to miss the chance to dramatize, Allen delivered a short "harangue" to his troops before moving to the attack. A dozing sentry suddenly caught sight of men moving towards the fort, fired his musket and rushed inside to alarm the garrison. But the shot misfired, and Allen and his shouting followers followed hard upon the sentry's heels. Once inside, the men rushed towards the barracks and Allen and Arnold towards the officers' quarters. A half-dressed and wholly surprised Captain William Delaplace of the 26th Regiment, who was serving as fort commandant, demanded to know in whose name the fort had been broken into. Allen cried out in full voice, "In the name of the Great Jehovah, and the Continental Congress."[26] This remark may be purely apocryphal, but it was typical of the man. Truth was no deterrent to Allen, and the fact that he had neither a firm faith in Jehovah nor a commission from the Continental Congress would never have discouraged him from claiming the blessing of both. Equally typical was Arnold's request to Delaplace to "Give up your arms and you'll be treated like a gentleman,"[27] an undertaking which, in fact, Arnold could not have fulfilled. Struggling to maintain his dignity and his temper, Delaplace was in no position to argue or refuse, and the fort was surrendered. His men, including his lieutenant, two sergeants and forty-four soldiers were herded to the parade ground without their weapons, while the Green Mountain Boys, discovering the whereabouts of the garrison's rum supply, helped themselves without restraint. Allen looked upon the scene, if not with pleasure, at least with indulgence. In his *Narrative* he wrote, "The sun seemed to rise that morning with a superior lustre; and Ticonderoga and its dependencies smiled on its conquerors, who tossed about the flowing bowl, and wished success to Congress and the liberty and freedom of America."[28] Arnold, Delaplace and Lieutenant Feltham looked upon the scene with distaste.

As soon as his rear guard arrived under Seth Warner, Allen sent them down the lake to the ruin that was Crown Point. Warner took with him Captain Remember Baker and about 100 men. Like Allen, they met with no resistance. The British garrison, consisting of a sergeant and a mere handful of men, gave in with more grace than that at Ticonderoga. They had never expected to defend the fort; theirs had been the task of acting as caretakers of the government stores, rather than that of garrison.

The achievement of Allen and Warner had been uncomplicated and bloodless and rich in booty. Nearly two hundred cannon, several tons of musket balls, a warehouse full of boatbuilding materials and numerous barrels of pork and flour, all useful, even essential additions to the small stocks in the possession of the rebel forces, fell into Allen's hands. Important as this acquisition was, even more significant in the long run was the boost which the captures of Ticonderoga and Crown Point gave to rebel morale, and the opportunities they afforded the Americans for further operations along the Lake Champlain-Richelieu River entry into Canada. This had been the traditional invasion route for generations. Along the waters of the lake and river had passed Indians, Americans and British, all on their way to the life stream of Canada, the St. Lawrence. Both Ticonderoga and Crown Point, known in Canadian history as Carillon and St. Frédéric, had been built by the French as the outer works of Canada's defence system, and even though the official boundary line had been moved north by George III in 1763, the two forts were still the outer guardians of Canada's military security.

Whether or not Allen appreciated the full strategic importance of his victories, it was Arnold who was prepared to profit from them. Riled by the lack of respect accorded him and his Massachusetts commission by the undisciplined "Bennington Mob," he hastened to explain to his superiors in Boston that he, not Allen, had been the real author of the seizure of Ticonderoga, and then set out to prove his military superiority over his rival. When some of his recruits arrived from Massachusetts, having captured Colonel Philip Skene's schooner, now given the name *Liberty*, Arnold embarked and set off for St. Jean, on the Richelieu. He had heard that there was a king's sloop at St. Jean and that she was loaded with stores. To capture her would be a neat coup and one for which he could claim full and unquestioned credit. To go to St. Jean meant to violate the Canadian frontier; but such political niceties were no deterrent to a determined man. Battling contrary winds, Arnold reached his destination and landed in a small creek "infested with numberless swarms of gnats and muskitoes."[29] After reconnoitring his position he realized that the British garrison, informed though they may have been of what had happened to their comrades in arms at Ticonderoga, were wholly unconscious of the fact that they might soon suffer the same fate. Completely taken aback at Arnold's sudden appearance, they gave in without firing a shot. Arnold thereupon seized the sloop and its cargo, burned several bateaux he could not take with him, and re-embarked. On his return journey he met Allen and his men laboriously rowing their heavy boats along the lake. Allen, too, was on his way to St. Jean, but he had been unable to catch up to Arnold's schooner. Arnold could now afford to be generous. He greeted Allen with a cannon salute, several "loyal Congress healths," and advice not to continue any further with his project.

Allen, however, was not to be persuaded. What Arnold had done he could do better. He therefore pushed on until May 18th when his men, weary-muscled with rowing, reached St. Jean. Here he paused to address a letter to the "Merchants that are friendly to the cause of Liberty in Montreal," informing them of his exploits on Lake Champlain and asking them to forward "Provisions, Ammunition and Spirituous Liquors" to St. Jean for the use of his army, "not as a Donation," but as a cash sale for five hundred pounds. He assured them that he was under instructions "not to contend with or in any way molest the Canadians or Indians" and that he was looking forward to an interview with them.[30]

At this point Allen apparently encountered the Montreal merchant, Joseph Bindon, who told him that Colonel Templer, the commander of the British garrison in Montreal, having learned of Arnold's raid, had ordered a detachment of the 26th Regiment to hasten to St. Jean under Major Charles Preston. Thus forewarned, Allen prepared to set up an ambuscade for the British troops. Meanwhile, Bindon, hurrying back towards Montreal with Allen's letter, met Preston. The British officer questioned him, but assured that he was carrying important papers to Colonel Templer, allowed him to continue his journey. The Americans, meanwhile, had given up the ambush plans, and, when Preston arrived, were in the process of re-embarking. There was a short exchange of shots, a couple of men were wounded and one American was taken prisoner; the remainder made off in their boats. Preston was angry. So too were his troops. They were now thoroughly convinced that Bindon had known all about the proposed ambuscade and that he had deliberately deceived them as to his mission. When some of the soldiers returned to Montreal they seized him and took him to the pillory in the market place. Some were even for hanging him. But Bindon had a glib

Benedict Arnold, from an anonymous English mezzotint published by Thomas Hart in 1776, showing Quebec in the background. Benedict Arnold's volatile temperament made him an aggressive commander of American troops.

tongue, and after persuading the magistrates that, although he might be guilty of imprudence he was not guilty of dishonesty, he was allowed to go free with a caution. Bindon, and the so-called Friends of Liberty, including Thomas Walker who had already entered into correspondence with Arnold to furnish him with military information rather than provisions, were pleased with what had happened, but not so those whom the Montreal notary, Simon Sanguinet, designated as "the honest men."[31]

Faced with the choice of condemning or condoning the actions of Allen and Arnold, the members of the Continental Congress did neither. At least not for the time being. Instead, they drafted and translated another letter to the people of Canada, couched in much the same words as those in the previous letter of October. There was the same talk of despotism and tyranny, the same exaltation of freedom, the same appeal to the courage and valour of the Canadians, the same assurance of friendship and the same threat of treating the Canadians as "enemies" should they fail to join the Americans in the defence of their "mutual liberty."[32] Everybody seemed to be writing letters. The Provincial Congresses of New York and New Hampshire penned similar documents to the Canadians to assure them that the Americans harboured no aggressive intentions against their persons or their property, the sole American aim being the liberation of Canada from the British. Allen and Arnold likewise tried to prove that the pen was as mighty as the sword by writing letters to Montreal, to the Caughnawaga Indians and to the Provincial Congresses of New York and Massachusetts, each endeavouring to enlist support, and each independently offering to

Fort St. Frédéric (Crown Point) in 1759, from a contemporary sketch by Thomas Davies.

conquer Canada if given the tools with which to do it.

At first Congress vacillated. But if, in May, there was some disposition to listen to suggestions that Ticonderoga and Crown Point should be given back to the British and the actions of Allen and Arnold disavowed, in June the delegates to the Philadelphia Congress were won completely to the idea of a full scale invasion of Canada. The clinching argument was the strategic one. To restore Ticonderoga and Crown Point would give the British a spring-board for an attack upon New York and the upper colonies; to retain them in American hands would be the best means of spoiling the malevolent British plans, and to seize Montreal would most effectively kill any British counter-revolutionary actions. What if the British were already thinking of pushing south along the Richelieu-Lake Champlain route to the Hudson; would not such a move cut the colonies in two and isolate New England? Would an attack on Canada be difficult? Allen and Arnold had each offered to conquer Canada with no more than 1500 or 2000 men. And were there not the friends of liberty in Canada ready to give aid and comfort to an American liberation army? Press forward to the conquest of Canada; it would give "the *coup de grace* to the hellish junto" that ruled in Great Britain and open the way for new men and new measures![33]

On June 13th Arnold drafted an invasion plan. St. Jean and Chambly could be invested by seven hundred men, three hundred more could defend the line of communications, and a major force of one thousand could bypass the Richelieu forts and drive straight to Montreal where the gates would be opened by the friends of Congress inside the walls. With Montreal in American hands, St. Jean, Chambly and Quebec would surrender in short order. Without massive reinforcements from Great Britain there was nothing Carleton could do. Military action would thus be the means, not only of "restoring that solid peace and harmony between Great Britain and her Colonies, so essential to the well-being of both," but also of gaining for the Americans the control of the "inexhaustible Granary" of Canada, the triangle between the Richelieu and the St. Lawrence, and forestalling any possibility of a British counter-attack upon New York on the Lake Champlain front.

This reasoning appealed to the members of Congress. It also appealed to the new commander in chief whom Congress had named, George Washington. But although Congress was ready to trust Arnold's arguments and plans, they were not ready to entrust him with the responsibility of putting them into effect. On June 27th Congress committed itself to the invasion of Canada but gave the command of the invading army not to Arnold, the "horse-jockey," but to Philip Schuyler, the New York patroon. Schuyler lacked Arnold's dynamism, but he possessed dignity, blue-blood and one of the largest landed estates in New York. That he was, at his age, better qualified to lead a quadrille than an undisciplined mob of men apparently made no difference to Congress.

In mid-July Schuyler set out for Ticonderoga. When he arrived, on the 18th, he found everyone, including the sentries, sound asleep. For the present, nothing could be done in the direction of aggressive action. First he would have to bring order out of administrative confusion, instill discipline into his raw and unreliable levies, and obtain information from the spy, John Brown, whom he sent to Montreal under the guise of "buying Canadian horses for the American market." For that reason it was not until August 30th that the northern army was more or less ready, and September 2nd before it encamped on Canadian soil. The Canadians were about to be brought into the continental union by force, because the Americans could not conceive of their enjoying life, liberty and the pursuit of happiness unless they were.

IV. Canada Prepares to Meet the American Invasion

The governor of Canada first learned on May 20th from Moses Hazen, an American of Jewish extraction who had served under Wolfe during the Seven Years' War and had purchased a small seigneury near St. Jean, of the nefarious activities of Allen and Arnold. Promptly turning over the administration of the province to his lieutenant governor, Hector Cramahé, Carleton hurried to Montreal. Following him went the fusiliers of the 7th Regiment under Major the Honourable Joseph Stopford, and a detachment

Major General Philip Schuyler who was appointed to command the American invasion of Canada via the Richelieu river in 1775, but who was obliged to yield his command to Richard Montgomery.

of the Royal Artillery with their field pieces and their ammunition. In Montreal, where he set up his headquarters, Carleton turned his immediate attention to strengthening his position. A quick survey of his resources showed him that of the three regiments under his command, one, the 8th, was beyond reach, scattered in the posts of the far west, while the men of the 7th and 26th were divided between St. Jean, Chambly, Lachine, Montreal and St. Francis. Carleton described it accurately when he reported to London, "not six hundred Rank and File fit for Duty upon the whole Extent of this great River, not an armed Vessel, no Place of Strength; the ancient Provincial Force enervated and broke to Pieces; all Subordination overset, and the Minds of the People poisoned by the same Hypocrisy and Lies practised with so much Success in the other Provinces."[34] For the moment there were no prospects of reinforcements from Great Britain; what additional troops he might obtain would have to be drawn from the local population. But while the gentry showed their usual zeal, and some of the young bloods offered their services as volunteers to go to St. Jean under Captain Mackay, nobody else seemed willing to come forward. Carpenters and boatbuilders might be hired to assist in repairing the works of the Richelieu forts and in constructing river transports, but where were the soldiers to come from? The people generally, according to Sanguinet who was an eye-witness of what went on in Montreal, showed themselves to be "badly disposed."[35] Even the publication on May 22nd of a *mandement* by Bishop Briand of Quebec elicited little more response than the accusation that the Bishop had sold out to the English government. The *mandement* praised George III for the concessions he had made to the French Canadians in the Quebec Act, and urged the habitants to pay no attention to American propaganda. Those who did not heed the bishop's instructions would risk denial of the sacraments and even the right to burial in consecrated ground.

As an answer to Carleton's problem, Sanguinet suggested to the governor that he re-establish the old French militia. This proposal did not meet with unqualified support, but Carleton was willing to take Sanguinet's advice. On June 9th he issued a proclamation, both in Montreal and Quebec, establishing martial law and calling out the militia "to the end . . . that so treasonable an invasion may be soon defeated, and all traitors with their . . . abetters, may be speedily brought to justice, and the publick peace and tranquillity of this province again restored, which the ordinary course of the civil law is at present unable to effect."[36] Carleton was none too optimistic about the outcome of his action, but, as he indicated in his letter to Dartmouth on the 26th, "what I shall be able to make of them, or of the Savages, I cannot positively say, but I am sure it is become highly necessary to try."[37]

Perhaps the efforts to assemble a militia force might have been more successful had the officers named to the senior appointments, the Baron de Longueuil, inspector of militia; Dufy-Desauniers, colonel; Neveu-Sevestre, lieutenant colonel; St. George Dupré, major in Montreal; and Voyer, colonel; Dumont, lieutenant colonel; and Dupré the elder, major, in Quebec, been less prone to fill the commissioned ranks with their friends and relatives.[38] Even more successful might his efforts have been had the governor made use of the captains of militia, instead of appealing to the noblesse. The fact is that Carleton had always placed too much reliance upon the noblesse. He overestimated their influence in the country and misunderstood the role which they had played in the old regime. They had fought nobly in the ranks of the regulars but had not commanded the militia; at no time had there ever existed a feudal obligation on the part of the censitaires to turn out in arms at the seigneurs' bidding. Thus, when Carleton sent his newly appointed officers into the back constituencies to raise the militia on the seigneuries, he was departing from and not following the traditional pattern of French Canadian military service. The results were unfortunate. In some places the officers were chased out of the parish, in others they were met with a solid wall of opposition. In Terrebonne, Lachenaie, Mascouche and Repentigny there was open resistance to the recruiting officers. The habitants felt they owed no traditional loyalty to the seigneurs and with improved crops and lower taxes they were too comfortable to want to join the armed services. Moreover, the ideas embodied in the Congress letters had aroused a certain interest among the more politically-minded among them.

The British merchants, too, provided no shining examples of loyalty to the Crown. A few of them, like Walker and Price, were actively engaged in treasonable correspondence with the enemy, and others were slow to come forward to prove their loyalty. Some expressed their willingness to fight should the need really arise and Montreal be invested, but refused to accept the commissions the governor was anxious to thrust upon them. In Quebec, in mid-July, one correspondent wrote to a friend in London, "we tryed here Yesterday to get the British Militia of this City and District to Assemble in order to form and have Officers Appointed but the very respectable number did not exceed seventy, thus you may see how the English Merchant Traders and Inhabitants are inclined." He added, "It is certain that all Winter the people of our Colonies have been corresponding with the Canadians and English people settled here and I am apt to think that is the cause of the present coolness."[39] Carleton, as incensed as he was worried about the situation, was inclined to agree with this statement. He could find excuses for the reluctance of the king's "new subjects" to transfer their unquestioning loyalty from Louis XV to George III, but he could find none for the king's "old subjects." They at least had the obligation of inspiring the French Canadians with their good example. He and Cramahé saw eye to eye on this matter, and both agreed that the indifference of the English merchants to military service could be traced to those "damn'd committees that had thrown the province into its present state and prevented the Canadians from taking arms."[40] In these circumstances the Earl of Dartmouth's instructions to Carleton to raise a body of 3000 Canadians must have brought forth a certain amount of hollow laughter.

But if Carleton could not raise a respectable militia, at least there was some hope of raising a regiment of provincial regulars. On April 3rd, George III had authorized Lieutenant Colonel Allan Maclean of Torloisk to raise a regiment among "our subjects who have, at different times emigrated from the North West parts of North Britain and have transported themselves, with their families, to New York." With his warrant Maclean went to Boston, where his scheme was endorsed by General Gage on June 12th. A number of former Highland soldiers, who had fought during the Seven Years' War, had settled in Canada, in Nova Scotia and in the Mohawk Valley, and from these men Maclean hoped to build his corps. The new regiment was to be known as the Royal Highland Emigrants and to be clothed like the Black Watch, except the sporran, which was to be of raccoon skin. Each man was to receive 200 acres of land, free of quit rent for twenty years. Maclean travelled to the Mohawk Valley, thence to Oswego and so to Canada, where he collected a body of men, chiefly disbanded soldiers from the Black Watch and Fraser's Highlanders. Here, at least, was a small reinforcement for Carleton's attenuated defence force. A less effective reinforcement came in the person of Brigadier General Richard Prescott, who was sent by Gage to assist Carleton.

In addition to the militia and the Emigrants, Carleton had reason to anticipate help from the Indians. The Six Nations had fought on the British side during the Seven Years' War and in the last stages of the conflict the Caughnawaga and the other Indians of the Seven Nations of Canada had thrown in their lot with Amherst as he moved ponderously towards Montreal. General Gage had spoken of the military potential of the Indians in September 1774, and Carleton, although never very enthusiastic about the Indians as military auxiliaries, wrote to the post commanders at Detroit, Kaskaskia, and Michillimackinac, telling them to look to their defences and to ensure the continued loyalty of the Indians to the British cause.

Of more immediate concern to Carleton was the loyalty of the Indians nearer home. It had always been British policy to placate the Indians, while exploiting them, when the need arose, as military auxiliaries. In order to retain their continued support, the British had sought not only to keep them supplied with arms, but also to shield them from the corrupt practices and unfair dealings of unscrupulous fur traders from the colonies. There is no doubt that the complaints of the Indians about "the abuses and irregularities of trade" in the Indian Territory, set up in 1763, were a strong influence in convincing the British to make the boundary changes that proved to be such an unpopular feature of the Quebec Act among the American colonists. This Act may be seen, therefore, not only as an effort on the part of the British to gain the loyalty of the king's "new subjects," but also as one designed to ensure and retain the traditional support of the king's Indian allies.

For many years the dominant influence among the Indians of the Iroquois Confederacy had been that of Sir William Johnson. Johnson's death in the summer of 1774 was a serious blow to the British position, if only because the Americans, through the agency of non-conformist missionaries, were making headway, particularly among the Oneida and the Tuscarora, in alienating "the affections of the Indians" and spiriting "them to bad purposes."[41] Nevertheless, the influence of the Johnson name was still strong and no one challenged the appointment of Sir William's nephew, Colonel Guy Johnson, as the Indians' choice for their Superintendent. Moreover, the selection of Joseph Brant as Guy's secretary strengthened Johnson's position, if only because it assured the continuance of the Johnson-Brant alliance of Sir William's day.

For the moment, the Indians remained quiet, watching and waiting for directions from Johnson. Then came the startling news of Lexington and the capture of Ticonderoga by Ethan Allen. The Indians were alarmed. So too was Guy Johnson. When rumours reached him that the New Englanders were planning to seize him and hold him prisoner, he left his home in the Mohawk Valley, and in company with several officers of the Indian Department and a few Mohawk chiefs, set out for Canada. At Ontario (now Oswego, New York) he held a conference which was attended by some 1450 Indians and 100 officers of the Indian Department. There he endeavoured to counter some of "the Vilianious Stories" and "false reports" which were being circulated by the more radical elements of the colonial population, and tried to "fix the Indians heartily in the Interests of the Crown."[42] According to the Indians, he did not ask them to take up the hatchet, rather he urged them to remain neutral while not forgetting their obligations to King George III. Then, with an escort of 220 Indians, he continued on his way to

Montreal, where he hoped to hold a conference with the Seven Nations of Canada.

Prior to this meeting, Daniel Claus of the Indian Department visited the Caughnawaga at Sault St. Louis. They told him of their "consternation and Alarm" at the rebel actions and of their own indecision as to how to act. They knew that Carleton was angry with them, and asked Claus to give them a full statement of the facts. In reply Claus outlined the "care, indulgence and protection" the Crown had always afforded the Indians and the "ungrateful behaviour" of the Americans; he referred to the aggressive actions of the colonists at Lexington and the "unwarrantable and rebellious Invasion" of Canada. He stressed the "ill usage" Indians had so frequently experienced at the hands of the colonists and pointed out what he called "the striking example" of Indian slavery in the colonies. These and "several more touching arguments" had the desired effect. The Indians were so "struck and roused" that they "determined of attacking and laying waste the New England Frontiers." Claus, however, advised them "to declare their sentiments first to the Governor at a public Congress to be held at Montreal in a few days" and meanwhile to warn the New Englanders "off their Territory at Crown Point and Tiyondaragon, and if they refused, to acquaint them with their Resolutions."[43]

The "public Congress" to which Claus had referred, met at Lachine on July 26th. According to contemporary count the Indians assembled there numbered 1664. They were still very much under the impact of their meeting with Claus and readily reiterated the aggressive proposals they had made to him. Carleton, however, merely thanked them for their goodwill and suggested that forty or fifty of them might go to St. Jean "to have a Lookout from the Garrison & watch the Motions of the Rebels at Crownpoint." He made it quite clear that they were under no circumstances to penetrate beyond the frontier of Quebec. This was not what the Indians wanted; neither was it what Guy Johnson had hoped for. He did his utmost to convince Carleton that this was not the way to handle the Indians, that it was essential "to keep up their Spirit and encourage on that Subject." But Carleton's orders were precise. Whether it was from political or humanitarian motives is not clear, but the governor flatly refused to loose the Indians on the frontiers of New England in the traditional Canadian manner.

"Something disgusted," as Claus puts it, a group of Indians set off for the frontier under François Thomas de Verneuil de Lorimier. On August 22nd, near the Lacolle River, they encountered an American reconnoitring party which had made its way into Canada and was returning with information about the forts at St. Jean and Chambly. In an exchange of shots, several Indians were wounded and the American leader, one of Allen's roistering companions, Remember Baker, was killed. The Indians went through his pockets, discovered his journal and other papers, cut off his head and took them all back triumphantly to St. Jean. Neither Carleton, nor his new military assistant General Prescott, seem to have profited much from the information the Indians had discovered; but the Americans moved quickly enough. Several pro-Congress Stockbridge Indians were sent hurriedly to Caughnawaga to assure the Canadian Indians that it had never been the intention of any American "to pluck one hair from an Indian's head, or to spill one drop of Indian blood."[44] For the present the Caughnawaga and Mohawk continued to send out scouting parties under officers of the Indian Department, including Gilbert Tice, Walter Butler and Sir William Johnson's son, Peter Johnson. But scouting held little attraction for men interested in fighting and the Indians began to grow restless. Some of the Onondaga and St. Regis Indians began to drift homewards; others were content to hang around Montreal filling their bellies with rum and their ears with sedition. At least that was how Guy Johnson saw it when he wrote in his journal, "For some time past, notwithstanding all the cares to prevent it, some of the Inhabitants continued to sell liquor to the Indians and to strip them of their cloathing, propagating also many dangerous reports among them, and telling them they approved of the rebells coming, as it was for the interest of the Colony."[45] Finally, after some months, even Johnson, Brant and Claus grew weary. They had no use for Carleton's do-nothing policy and set sail for England. Just before his departure, without consulting Carleton, Johnson gave the Indians of Lorette a belt to be forwarded through all the Indian Nations "to keep them steady to their Engagements" while he was gone.

Carleton addressed himself to another responsibility, that of strengthening the fixed fortifications along the expected invasion route. Nothing could be done about Ticonderoga and Crown Point; both had been lost to the enemy early in May. Nor was it possible to do much about Montreal, which possessed only a weak stone wall and an inadequate citadel. The obvious thing was to look at the gateway to the province, Fort St. Jean, standing just to the north of the frontier and badly needing attention. From the standpoint of public morale, Carleton knew that he would have to fight his battles as near to the frontier as possible; he could not afford to yield too much territory to the invader, to retire to Montreal or to Quebec. Moreover, St. Jean had certain obvious advantages. It was connected with Montreal by road by way of Laprairie; it could not be easily by-passed by an invading force intent upon capturing Montreal; and its location on the river provided a base from which vessels might sail to intercept any invasion force while still on Lake Champlain. Close by St. Jean was Chambly, which, even if it were defended by a thin stone wall proof only against musket fire, would serve as an easily accessible supply depot. It was Carleton's strategy, therefore, to repair the fortifications of St. Jean, to garrison it with as strong a contingent of regulars as he could afford and as many Canadian volunteers as he could find, and to provide it with as many watercraft as could be constructed. Thus, should the invaders fail to put in an appearance or be hurled back,

Colonel Guy Johnson, leader of the Confederate Indians who supported the British during the American Revolution. Oil on canvas, by Benjamin West (1738-1820).

Carleton would be ready to launch his own attack from St. Jean to recover the former British forts, Crown Point and Ticonderoga.

Time was the important factor. Carleton would have to move fast. He did not doubt that the enemy would be back again; they had said they would. In fact, two of the vessels taken by Arnold in May poked their bows across the horizon on June 7th and fired a few shots before withdrawing up river to the safety of the lake. The actual work on the defences was left to the Royal Engineer, Captain John Marr. The fort had originally consisted of two earthern redoubts, one around the barrack block in which the troops were housed, and the other around a handsome stone house. Marr decided to join these redoubts together with a communication line defended by a palisade and to surround the whole, except on the river side, with a ditch seven feet deep. This would facilitate movement within the fort in relative safety. He also constructed a line of projecting pickets along the outer base of the walls to discourage a frontal attack by assault infantry.[46] Into this reasonably strong but rather makeshift work Carleton thrust a military force made up of 474 infanteers of the 7th and 26th Regiments of Foot, 90 Canadians, volunteers and militiamen, 38 gunners of the Royal Artillery, and 20 Highlanders from Maclean's Royal Highland Emigrants, or 662 men all told. The military garrison was commanded by Major Charles Preston; Lieutenant William Hunter of H.M. brigantine *Gaspé* was there to build the river fleet which, by the time the enemy arrived, included a schooner, *Royal*

Savage, and two unfinished row galleys. The small force of Canadians was commanded by Sieur de Belestre, an experienced partisan leader during the Seven Years' War, and former commandant of Detroit. A small patrol of Indians, based upon St. Jean, was under the charge of Lorimier and Gilbert Tice.

Despite his efforts to assume a posture of defence, Carleton was in a weak position when the American invasion began early in September. He was paying the penalty for mistakes of judgement not of his own making; his superiors had for too long neglected advice to maintain the lake forts in good repair and strength, and then, with trouble threatening in Massachusetts, had deprived him of half of his disposable regular troops. But he suffered too from mistakes that were of his own making. Had he not placed too much reliance upon support from within Canada, and for too long tolerated the sedition that spread from Montreal throughout the province? Now he was going to have to face the enemy with virtually all his regulars concentrated in St. Jean and with only an unreliable militia to defend the rest of the country. He was unlikely to get reinforcements, at least in 1775. His request for two regiments from Boston had been turned down by a weak and cautious Vice Admiral of the Royal Navy, the inefficient Samuel Graves, who refused to push his frigate *Cerberus* or any transports up the St. Lawrence because he considered it an "extremely dangerous" and "impracticable" operation with the year so far advanced.[47] Everything would therefore depend upon holding St. Jean. If the Richelieu fort surrendered, Montreal would have to go; and there would remain only Quebec, standing boldly and defiantly on its rocky cliffs, a hollow shell of a fortress, bare of the troops that were its life and the guns that were its strength — an invitation to any ambitious enemy commander.

Guy Carleton's coach, at the Canadian War Museum. This vehicle, dating from c. 1775, was used by Carleton while he was in Canada. The body is hung on "Cee" springs and strong leather braces to give more comfort when riding over Canadian roads.

II The Montreal Campaign 1775

I. The American Invasion Begins

The American invasion of 1775 was a two-pronged affair. The left wing, based upon Ticonderoga and Crown Point, was to push north along the Champlain-Richelieu route towards Montreal and the St. Lawrence. This operation had been approved by Congress in June and was under the command of Philip Schuyler and his chief lieutenant, Richard Montgomery, a former British officer who had settled in New York after the Seven Years' War and married into a strong rebel family, the Livingstons. The troops comprised contingents from Massachusetts, Connecticut and New York, numbering, all told, in the vicinity of 3000 men. The right wing, led by Benedict Arnold, who, having failed to secure an appointment under Schuyler, had come up with a scheme for the invasion of Canada by another American army travelling by way of the Kennebec River, over the height of land and into Canada by way of the Chaudière. This route had been much less travelled than that in front of Schuyler. It had been used on occasions by the Indians during the Ancien Régime, but it had not been surveyed until 1761, when the task was undertaken by a British military engineer, John Montresor. The original idea of a military operation by way of the Kennebec seems to have been made first by one Jonathan Brew. It was, however, Arnold who pressed the idea and aroused the interest of George Washington in the possibility of drawing British troops away from the Richelieu River and thus making progress to Montreal much easier for Schuyler. Once Arnold's plan had received Washington's support, Congress was ready to give its blessing and authorized the recruiting of men in Pennsylvania, Maryland and Virginia. Both Schuyler's troops and Arnold's set out for Canada by different routes at much the same time and with much the same numbers, although there does not appear to have been any well worked-out schedule or definite plans for concerted action other than occasional letters exchanged by courier over miles of wilderness. Thus Montgomery, with 1500 men, set out from Crown Point on August 30th on the first leg of the

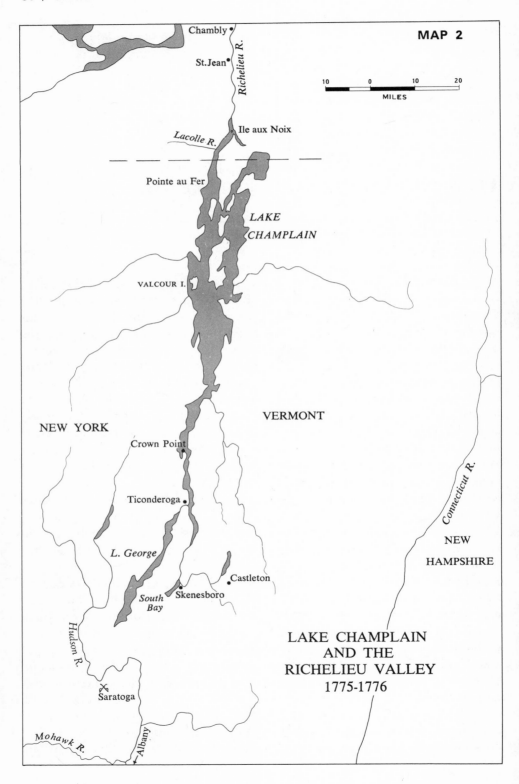

MAP 2

Chambly

St.Jean

Richelieu R.

10 0 10 20
MILES

Lacolle R.

Ile aux Noix

Pointe au Fer

LAKE
CHAMPLAIN

VALCOUR I.

VERMONT

NEW YORK

Crown Point

Ticonderoga

Connecticut R.

NEW

HAMPSHIRE

L. George

Castleton

South
Bay

Skenesboro

Hudson R.

Saratoga

LAKE CHAMPLAIN
AND THE
RICHELIEU VALLEY
1775-1776

Mohawk R.

Albany

campaign in western Quebec; while Arnold left Cambridge, Massachusetts, twelve days later with 1200 men, on the overland march to Quebec. Both men had their eyes on the St. Lawrence and both expected to achieve the conquest of Canada before the year was out.

Schuyler was a sick man when he joined Montgomery at Ile aux Noix on September 4th. Rheumatism was in his bones and fever was in his blood; nevertheless he was determined to lead his troops into action. Leaving a small rear party behind him, he embarked his men in their clumsy flatboats and pushed on down the Richelieu River. At a distance of about two miles from St. Jean the gunners in the fort sighted the American boats and hurled a few shells in their direction. Undeterred, the flatboats approached another mile and then turned in towards the left bank of the river. Preston's *Royal Savage* had put in no appearance and the whole operation had all been much easier than Schuyler had expected. The Americans landed in a swampy area and, forming up by companies, began to march in the direction of the fort. Suddenly, with no warning, gunfire blazed in their faces. A fighting patrol of about one hundred Indians[1] led by Lorimier and Captain Gilbert Tice of the Indian Department, had been waiting concealed in the bush for just such an opportunity. But the Americans were no novices in the tricks of Indian warfare; they wheeled to the left, and took to cover. The sniping continued for some time and then, towards evening, the Americans built a breastwork. This work, however, afforded no protection once the gunners of the fort found the range and the Americans were compelled to withdraw. This engagement, of no great significance from a military standpoint, had an adverse effect upon the Indians. They had lost not only Tice, who was wounded, but also four of their own men killed and four wounded, and while they claimed it as a victory, they bitterly resented the fact that the soldiers behind the walls of the fort had made no effort to come to their assistance. They, the Indians, had borne the brunt of the fighting and they did not like it. If this was what they were to expect in the future, they would take more care not to expose their own skins when the white men were going to take such care of theirs.

At this point Moses Hazen, who seems to have been playing the role of double agent or trimmer, at this stage, visited Schuyler in the dark of night.[2] The picture he presented was dark and forbidding. The fort at St. Jean was well defended, plentifully supplied with cannon and troops, and *Royal Savage* was almost ready to take to the river at any time. Moreover, Hazen doubted the willingness of the Canadians to offer any support to the Americans. This last information was particularly significant, as Schuyler had been led to believe that the Canadians would be more than sympathetic and his expedition had been predicated upon such support. Hazen's report was considered at a council of war the next morning and the decision was taken to withdraw. Ill, worn and haggard, Schuyler made his way back to Ile aux Noix, where he took up his pen and scratched a note to Congress, "Should

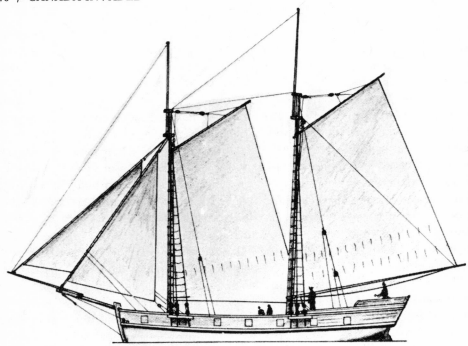

The schooner *Royal Savage* which was used both by the British in 1775 and by the Americans in 1776 following her capture at St. Jean.

we not be able to do anything decisively in Canada, I shall judge it best to move from this place, which is a very wet and unhealthy part of the Country, unless I receive orders to the contrary."[3]

Scarcely had Schuyler arrived at Ile aux Noix when he received new and conflicting intelligence about the Canadians. This came from James Livingston, an American who had settled at Chambly and who was related to Montgomery's wife. According to Livingston, Hazen had misjudged the attitude of the habitants. How could the French Canadians be expected to support the American troops, if there were no American troops to support? He urged Schuyler to make another effort to besiege St. Jean, promising that Canadian help would be forthcoming. Schuyler agreed to make the effort. Reinforcements were steadily making their way down the lake to Ile aux Noix, and his force was now up to 1900 men. However, a goodly proportion of them complained of malaria and promptly took to their tents, and when Montgomery set out again for St. Jean on the 10th, he had with him a force about 1000 strong. The Americans returned without interruption to the breastwork they had constructed, and then Montgomery detached a large contingent, under Lieutenant Colonel R. Ritzema, to make its way through the woods and set up a post below the fort, thus severing Preston's line of communication with Laprairie and Montreal. But the Americans were jittery. The silence was almost as sinister as the sound of Indian warwhoops and the slightest sound or movement seemed to chill their bones as it robbed them of their reason; before too long Ritzema's men began firing at their comrades, mistaking them for the enemy. When this slight matter of identification was straightened out, there was another skirmish, this time with real Indians. Montgomery held his position but when the rumour began to circulate that *Royal Savage* was on its way, its brass and iron cannon ready to blast them from their position, the Americans took to their heels. Montgomery had some difficulty in rounding them up, but none at all in inducing them to go on board their boats and in getting them to push off once again for Ile aux Noix.[4] The 13th — date of ill-omen — was picked for another attempt against St. Jean; but the weather intervened, and on the 16th, the prostrate Schuyler, now under the healing care of his wife who had been summoned from Ticonderoga, was carried in a litter and placed on board a vessel setting out for Lake Champlain. Schuyler was, of course, to recover his health and to make his contribution to his army in an administrative capacity, but he never returned again to lead it in siege or in battle.

On the same day, the 16th, Montgomery returned to St. Jean with his invasion troops. He might deplore their lack of discipline, their laziness and their malingering, and call them the "worst stuff imaginable for soldiers," but at least they were increasing daily in numbers and were about 2000 strong. Better still, he now had a navy consisting of a schooner, a sloop, two row galleys, each with a 12 pounder cannon, and ten bateaux. It was not a large fleet, but it was large enough to blockade the Richelieu River and prevent *Royal Savage* from breaking out of the river and sailing around Lake Champlain to intercept supplies and reinforcements moving to Montgomery's assistance. In addition, he had managed to pick up a few Canadians. They had been recruited in the vicinity of Chambly by Livingston and by Jeremy Duggan, a former barber from Quebec, and about forty of them were serving under Major John Brown.

Despite sporadic shelling from the fort, the Americans disembarked and began to take up positions encircling the fort on the left bank of the river. Swinging around to the north, Brown succeeded in capturing a small British supply train bringing provisions to the fort, and in setting himself up in an old British redoubt astride the line of communications to Laprairie and Montreal. Preston saw the danger of his situation and set a fighting patrol to oust Brown. After a sharp engagement, Brown was forced to pull back, but before the British could consolidate their position Montgomery had descended upon them with 500 men. The British withdrew in good order, suffering several casualties, but regaining the cover of St. Jean without losing cohesion and bringing with them, as a prisoner, Moses Hazen, whom they had found with Brown.[5] Thus, by the evening of September 18th the Americans held the whole of the left bank around St. Jean. They were ready to begin the siege. Preston had no illusions about the perils of his situation and sent the Indian leader, Lorimier, through the American lines to inform Carleton of what might be expected if no relief arrived.

The Americans did not stand still at St. Jean waiting for the walls to collapse before their bugle calls. Montgomery was too experienced an officer for that. While continuing his envelopment of the fortress he sent detachments towards Montreal to keep an eye on Carleton's movements. Brown was ordered to establish a post at Laprairie and Ethan Allen to pick up a few Canadian partisans and then to go to Longueuil, opposite Montreal on the south shore of the St. Lawrence. Meanwhile Livingston and Duggan, with the assistance of Loizeau, a blacksmith from Chambly, were to drum up more recruits among Canadians in the neighbourhood of Pointe Olivier. Livingston had sent a letter on September 16th through the parishes around Chambly, inviting the French Canadians to furnish the Americans with flour, for which he promised prompt payment and suggesting that they demonstrate their "fraternal friendship" with the invaders by joining "as a militia." On the 18th Livingston repeated his request, urging the Canadians to come to his new camp at Pointe Olivier "with your arms to protect our flanks, which are menaced by people seeking our slavery," and assuring them that the Americans were animated only by "spiritual good" in entering into "paternal correspondence" with the Canadians.[6]

The more substantial farmers and officers of the local militia did not take this specious propaganda very seriously and endeavoured to persuade their friends and neighbours to resist Livingston's blandishments. So far were they successful that the parish of St. Denis sent a request to Carleton asking him to pardon their lack of enthusiasm for the government. Carleton, who had become a little sour at the failure of the Canadians to respond to his appeal — he told Godefroy de Tonnancour at Trois Rivières on September 6th that the only Canadian he had seen under arms on behalf of the Crown had been the sentry at Tonnancour's door[7] — immediately acquiesced, writing a note of pardon and sending it to St. Denis by a prominent French Canadian merchant from Montreal, the Sieur Jean Aurillac. Livingston's men, however, got wind of Aurillac's mission. They attacked the curé's house at St. Denis where Aurillac had taken refuge, fired a bullet through a window which killed, unfortunately, the curé's female servant, made prisoners of the frightened Aurillac and one Leveillé (who had been a volunteer at St. Jean), and sent both under guard to the Thirteen Colonies.[8] The loyalists at St. Denis were indignant and expected that Carleton would respond at once to this insult. To their surprise and consternation the governor made no move. He would not abandon the shelter of the walls of Montreal. There seems little doubt that Carleton's inaction, the better part of valour though it may have been, led many French Canadians to wonder whether the British days in Canada were numbered. Apparently they had nothing to lose, and perhaps something to gain by co-operating with the rebel army; and while they debated with themselves, they made no effort to hinder Livingston's plans to intercept any British vessel attempting to move up or down the Richelieu between Sorel, Chambly and St. Jean.

General Richard Montgomery, the former British officer who commanded the invasion force which captured Montreal in 1775, and who was killed during the assault on Quebec.

A sketch of a French Canadian Habitant in winter costume, by F. von Germann.

II. Guy Carleton Captures Ethan Allen

Meanwhile the impetuous Allen rushed once more to the forefront of the historical stage. The captor of Ticonderoga had quarrelled with his cousin, Seth Warner, over the leadership of the Green Mountain Boys and had, in consequence, found himself without a commission and without an army in the war which he had practically started single-handed. Schuyler had no desire to have anything to do with him. Finally, however, he agreed to accept Allen as a "volunteer." "I always dreaded," the American general wrote to John Hancock, "his impatience of subordination and it was not until after solemn promise made me in the presence of several officers that he would demean himself properly that I would permit him to attend the army; nor would I have consented then, had not his solicitations been backed by several officers."[9] Allen therefore accompanied Brown to St. Jean. He claimed in his *Narrative* that he had assisted Montgomery "in laying a line of circumvallation round the fortress" of St. Jean, but Montgomery was as anxious to get rid of him as Schuyler had been, and that was why Allen was sent on a roving mission "preaching politics," or in other words preaching sedition into the ears of the Canadian population and rallying them to the American cause.

At that point Allen conceived the idea of capturing Montreal. Perhaps a *coup de main* of the kind that had succeeded so well at Ticonderoga might achieve the same result at Montreal. It was not exactly what Montgomery had in mind for Allen to do. But Allen was always prone to lofty imaginings and he found in Brown, now at Laprairie, a patient listener. The two men apparently agreed that Brown with his 200 men would cross the St. Lawrence from south-west of the town and that Allen would go to Longueuil and cross the river at that point. This would bring him close to L'Assomption, where Thomas Walker, who might be of help, was now living since withdrawing from Carleton's reach in Montreal. It was further agreed that crossings would be effected during the night of September 24th. As a signal for the assault on the town, each force would give three loud huzzas when it arrived at its appointed station. In accordance with this plan Allen hurried back to Longueuil. Here he picked up a few men and with a mixed bag of Canadians and Americans, numbering about 110 in all, he paddled over the St. Lawrence towards Longue Pointe. Because they were short of boats his men were obliged to make several journeys before the whole contingent had arrived safely on the island of Montreal in the early hours of the morning. Then Allen waited, listening patiently, for the shouts of Brown's men. For reasons of his own, which remain obscure — lack of boats in which to cross the river or a misunderstanding of the details of Allen's plan — Brown did not move. He was still at Laprairie. Uncertain what to do, Allen sent a messenger to look for Brown, and another to Thomas Walker to ask for "speedy assistance."[10] For the first time he began to appreciate just how perilous his situation was, and endeavoured to maintain field security by prohibiting any movement from L'Assomption into Montreal. Meanwhile Walker hurried about, coaxing and bullying the local habitants into mustering to help Allen who, despite his bravado, had sufficient judgement to realize that he could hardly take Montreal with so small a force as that under his command. If his presence could be kept a secret he might manage to get back to Longueuil undetected. But Allen's security cordon was much too thin. A young habitant named Desautels had spotted the presence of the "Bastonnois" and had hurried to report his discovery to Guy Carleton while Allen was still wondering what to do.

Carleton had left Montreal for Quebec not long before Schuyler began his northward movement at the beginning of September. However, immediately he learned of the presence of enemy troops on Canadian soil, he suspended the sittings of the new Legislative Council, which had been appointed under the Quebec Act, arranged for his wife and children to be sent back to England, left Cramahé in charge of the administration, and hurried with all available troops from the capital to his headquarters in Montreal. With the assistance of Brigadier General Prescott he arranged for the posting of guards and for the enrolment of volunteers. At the same time he sent instructions to the rural parishes to muster fifteen men from each company and to get them under arms, an order which, incidentally, elicited very little response, particularly in those regions already occupied by the Americans and where the Canadian population was disposed to adhere to the rebel cause. News of the shooting of the Sieur Perthuis and the wounding of the Sieur de la Bruaire while fighting with the Indians against Montgomery at St. Jean had also acted as a damper upon the militia, and when the Sieur de Niverville was sent by Carleton to assist St. Jean with a small force of Indians and Canadians, he found his men incapable of or unwilling to try conclusions with Brown's Americans at Laprairie. It was clear that with an indifferent and disloyal population at his back, there was not much that Carleton could do at this time about sending assistance to the beleaguered garrison at St. Jean. "The Canadians w'd not march, a very inconsiderable number excepted, notwithstanding every effort has been tryed, and every argument used by the Clergy," wrote Carleton gloomily on September 21st, only the "better sort of Citizens, and Gentlemen of the Country." Even the Indians had, for the most part, stayed at home. All that could save Canada would be the despatch of "ten or twelve thousand men here, early next spring, completely equipped, with some frigates. . ."[11]

It was at this moment that Carleton was informed by Desautels of Allen's presence just outside the gates of Montreal. The people of the town had learned it too, even before Carleton, and their immediate response was one of consternation on the part of some and action on the part of others. Most of the French and English inhabitants rushed with their muskets to the Champ de Mars where Carleton "shew'd them in a few words the danger which threaten'd the town and the necessity of driving that Banditti back."[12] The drums beat sharply and the volunteers marched to the military barracks to receive an issue of powder and ball from the military stores. Meanwhile other inhabitants of the town had rushed with equal haste to the docks, dragging their wives and children with them and carrying their personal belongings to one or other of the vessels tied up at the wharves of Montreal. If Allen was going to occupy the town they were going to get away first, such was the terror his name inspired among the more timid members of the populace. Surprisingly enough neither Carleton nor Prescott marched with the volunteers. They remained in town ready to leave should Allen succeed.

The force which marched out the east gate of Montreal was led by Major John Campbell, recently appointed Superintendent of the Quebec Indians. It comprised 34 regulars of the 26th Regiment, 120 French Canadians, 80 English, 20 officers of the Indian Department and half a dozen Indians. As the troops neared the Truteau River, they discovered Allen waiting for them along the river bank, his men making good use of the cover afforded by the trees, rocks and farm buildings. Campbell responded by placing his regulars in the centre and extending his militia outwards on each flank. Duggan's Canadians, who occupied Allen's right flank, realized that they would be outflanked and fled into the woods. Allen's other flank did likewise, and

Governor Carleton reviewing his troops on Place D'Armes before attacking Ethan Allen at Longue Pointe — 1775.

although the big Green Mountain Boy, as LaNaudière wrote to his friend François Baby, conducted himself in action "with great valour,"[13] he, too, took to his heels when he realized the futility of further fighting. As he ran he was pursued by Peter Johnson, an officer of the Canadian Indian Department. Allen fired a few wild shots at Johnson and then turned around and surrendered his sword. Altogether the Montrealers took thirty-six prisoners, of whom sixteen were Canadians who told Carleton that they had been assured that the whole population of Montreal was with them and that they could expect to enter the town without opposition. For this they were to receive thirty pence per day. Instead, they had been involved in a fight they did not anticipate. Five of their force had been killed and ten others wounded. On the British side, Major John Carden, a member of the Legislative Council, was mortally wounded; so too was Alexander Paterson, a Montreal merchant. One soldier was killed. The Sieur Beaubassin, a French Canadian volunteer, and another soldier were both wounded.

The importance of the loyalist success on September 25th was to be found, not in the numbers of men killed and wounded, but in the effect that it had upon the people of the country. The Canadians saw, many of them, with their own eyes, the huge figure of Ethan Allen, clad in his coarse homespun clothes and his deerskin cap with its eagle feather, humbled and humiliated in defeat; they saw him marched to the ship in the harbour on which he was to embark on the first leg of his journey back to England to stand trial for treason to his rightful king, George III.[14] They saw, too, that, in the final analysis, French and English people in Canada were prepared to fight in defence of their land. Perhaps George III might, after all, prove to be stronger than Congress. In consequence, French Canadians crowded into Montreal from the outlying regions, anxious to join the militia they had spurned only days before; English merchants, too, who had been ready to listen to the seditious talk of Walker and Price — the latter had become an agent of Congress in the late summer — now decided that they ought to pledge themselves to defend their lives and property "against all such Invaders, their Adherents, Associates, Abbetters" and to "make the cause of each the General Cause of the Whole."[15]

To the more sanguine, military-minded leaders of the community, the time now seemed ripe to mount a relief expedition for St. Jean. Why not strike while the enthusiasm was hot, why delay until it had cooled? A relief force led by Carleton, combining with a sortie by Preston from the fort, might well compel Montgomery to withdraw to Ile aux Noix, perhaps farther. According to Sanguinet, some 1200 men came in from the rural districts, and these together with the 600 who could be mustered in Montreal, and the Indians from St. Regis and Two Mountains, would give

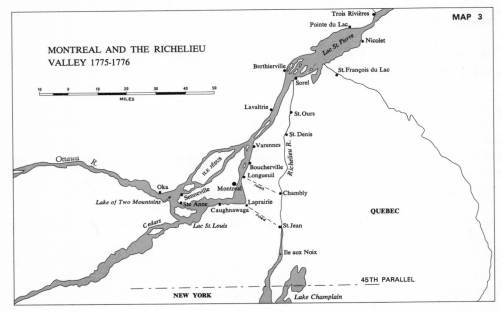

MAP 3

MONTREAL AND THE RICHELIEU
VALLEY 1775-1776

Carleton over 2000 fighting men. This force, surely, would be sufficient to give second thoughts to Montgomery. For several weeks the Canadians and Indians remained waiting and ready in Montreal, subsisting on the king's rations and wondering when Carleton would move. And then the rural militiamen began to drift away. They had their crops to attend to and what was even more critical, they had their own homes to protect against the marauding bands of Americans and disloyal Canadians, who were burning the houses and barns of those militiamen whose absence they attributed to service in the king's army.

Carleton did not remain wholly inactive. If he showed no stomach for fighting Montgomery, at least he felt sufficiently secure to take action against the main source of seditious activity in Montreal. Too long had Thomas Walker moved with impunity through the streets of Montreal, receiving enemy agents and encouraging the local population to support the American invaders. There was ample evidence against him. Carleton had in his possession copies of many of the letters which had passed between Walker and Brown and Allen and Arnold; and even if these letters were, most of them, of a period prior to the actual invasion, there were the affidavits of those French Canadians who had witnessed Walker's meetings with American officers, listened to his seditious talk and had been personally aware of his efforts to suborn the Canadian population. Men like Pierre Charland, Jean Baptiste Bruyères, Joseph Deschamps and Germain LeRoux were all aware of what was going on and were prepared to tell the British authorities.[16] Finally a warrant was issued for Walker's arrest, and on October 5th it was served on him at L'Assomption. But Walker did not give up easily. When Ensign John Macdonell and his small military party of Royal Highland Emigrants arrived and demanded his surrender, he fired at them, injuring Macdonell and a soldier, and continued, with his servants' help, to defend himself with his pistols. It was only when the soldiers set fire to his house that he submitted to arrest. Once in custody, Walker was, like Ethan Allen, marched to the dock at Montreal and placed in irons on board one of the vessels in the harbour. For this action Carleton was charged with brutality. In defence of himself he wrote to Dartmouth on October 25th pointing out that he had no alternative; "'tis true the Rebels have been in Irons, not from choice but necessity, we have neither Prisons to hold nor Troops to guard them, so that they have been treated with as much humanity, as our own safety wou'd permit."[17] A not unreasonable reply.

III. Major Charles Preston's Defence of Fort St. Jean

Meanwhile the siege of St. Jean had begun in earnest, accompanied by a hard and driving rain which set in on September 19th and which plagued both the garrison and the besiegers. Despite the fact that General Prescott had written to Preston urging him "to send out Detachments to harrass or attack the Enemy" and to consult the Canadian commander, Belestre,

Major (later Sir) Charles Preston, who defended Fort St. Jean against the Americans in 1775.

"upon the best manner of conducting them, as he is an Officer of experience and perfectly acquainted with the manner of carrying War in this Country,"[18] Preston preferred to rely largely upon his gunners. He had a good number of cannon in the fort and plenty of ammunition, and in this respect he enjoyed an advantage over the besiegers which he was able to exploit to the utmost. His tactics were, therefore, to clear a good field of fire in front of the redoubts by blowing up the buildings which obscured his view of the enemy positions, and by directing his long range guns upon the batteries erected by Montgomery's artillerymen to the north and south of the redoubts.

The following entries in Preston's journal tell, in bare and unadorned terms, the story of the warfare that was this siege: September 22nd, "a deserter came in, he told us the enemy were erecting a Battery close to the edge of the wood south of the redoubts, and within 400 yards of us. . . . We sent a good many Shot and shells to the place the deserter pointed out to us"; September 23rd, "A deserter came in this morning, he ascertains the place where the Enemy are erecting their Battery and we distress them as much as we can with Shells."[19] During the first weeks of the siege Preston's fire rate showed a preponderance over that of the Americans of something like ten to one; and the British enjoyed this advantage until such time as their opponents were able to bring more and heavier guns from Ticonderoga.

For a month the garrison of St. Jean lived a life of dank, unwholesome boredom. All the women and children attached to the garrison had been ordered to take refuge within the walls of the fort, thus bringing some thirteen hundred human beings within the muddy confines of the two redoubts. Occasionally the routine of daily shelling was broken by the arrival of a deserter from the American camp or the departure of a British deserter into the nearby woods, and by the despatch of an occasional patrol sent to check the movement of the besiegers. On some occasions Preston's bateaux would sail up the river and throw a few shells into the American position at close quarters; on others, *Royal Savage* would make a foray within the narrow limits available to her for manoeuvre on the Richelieu. On September 29th an Indian arrived with news of Allen's defeat and capture, news which was rendered less cheering by his statement that 4000 Canadians were "in Arms against us." With all these comings and goings the American blockade of St. Jean seems to have been loose enough; certainly no attempt was made to interfere with Captain Monin and Monsieur Moiquin when they went out on October 4th and drove eight head of cattle, grazing in the neighbouring fields, into the fort, to provide fresh meat for the occupants. Preston noted in his journal, "None of the Enemy happen'd to be near the Spot and they were not fir'd upon." The Americans were apparently absorbed in other activities, if we may judge from another entry, "We heard a great many Shouts amongst the Enemy and the sound of Axes at work."[20]

As the enemy brought in more and larger guns and mortars from the forts on Lake Champlain, the tempo and volume of their cannonade increased. One large mortar from Ticonderoga, known affectionately to the besiegers as the "Sow," was the occasion of humorous remarks both inside and outside St. Jean. But Preston was in no mood for fun when he entered in his journal, "we afterwards had reason to think that anything relating to the Sow was a better Joke on them than on us."[21] Although it is clear from Preston's account that the bombardment of St. Jean by the two American batteries on the west bank of the Richelieu resulted in remarkably few casualties, it is also clear that the bombardment was not without its serious

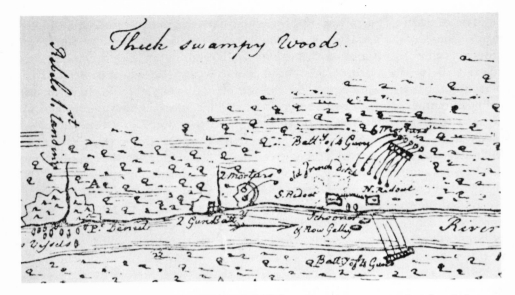

A contemporary sketch of the siege of St. Jean, 1775.

A British fusilier of the period of the invasion of Canada.

effects upon the morale of the defenders. How else is one to interpret Preston's entry on October 15th in his journal? He wrote, "The Weather grew very cold, and as the Windows of the house were all broke; as many as cou'd find room in the Cellars slept there. The rest unable either to get a place or to bear the heat and disagreeable smell arising from such numbers being crowded together slept above in cold and danger or walk'd about the greatest part of the night. Towards Evening we were again saluted with shells; and the night being cold and wet, it was thought proper to rouse us at Midnight with a few Shells and Shot."[22]

From Preston's standpoint, even more serious than the increased volume of shells hurled at the defences of St. Jean, was the discovery that the Americans had determined upon a manoeuvre which might well have been expected sooner. Early in October, Montgomery completed the envelopment of St. Jean by crossing the Richelieu River and opening up a new gun position on the east bank directly opposite the exposed part of the fort. Preston knew what to expect and sent a row galley, mounting a 24 pounder gun and commanded by an artillery officer, to discourage the American gunners. There was a sharp exchange between the men on the bateau and the American troops, and after several of their men had been wounded, including Dr. Millar, the Surgeon's Mate, the British became discouraged and withdrew. What made the new American battery so dangerous to Preston was not that it closed the open side of St. Jean through which scouts and messengers could slip undetected, so much as that it exposed Preston's river fleet to the direct fire of the American guns. Henceforth it would be impossible to move *Royal Savage*, or even the bateaux, without attracting the attention of the enemy and bringing down a volley of gun shot. Lieutenant William Hunter, the naval officer in charge of the fleet, made this point emphatically when he wrote to Preston, "I give it as my Opinion, that . . . there is no possibility of being out of range of the Enemy's Shot from their Batterys." In these circumstances Hunter recommended that all the vessels should be hauled "close to the Shore between the Redoubts, there if the Vessel's are sunk, their artillery and Store's will be saved, and the Vessel's at a proper opportunity may be weigh'd again."[23] Preston had no choice but to follow Hunter's advice and the several naval craft were immobilized close to the redoubts. However, no sooner was this operation completed than *Royal Savage* was caught in a volley of red hot shot and sunk to her ports. Unfortunately the sinking took place before Hunter had removed the brass ordnance from the schooner. The naval commander felt embarrassed when he wrote to Preston, "if Major Preston has no occasion for the Guns Mr. Hunter thinks they are safe there as any where, as it is impossible they can be carried off without the Centinels giving the alarm." One may assume that sharp words passed between the soldiers and the seamen over the sinking of *Royal Savage* and the failure to salvage her guns, when we read Hunter's postscript to his letter of the 17th, "Mr. Hunter must likewise hint to the Major that he has been many Years at Sea, that he can Rigg a Ship, Navigate, and Manoeuvre her, this is notorious to many in the Navy."[24] Inter-service arguments have never been limited to any one day or generation. Offended or not, Hunter had no other choice than to place himself and his men at Preston's disposal and to withdraw his seamen from the ships on which they had lived up to this time, to find whatever accommodation they could in the wretched buildings inside the walls of the fort.

About twelve miles north of St. Jean, at the carrying place on the Richelieu, stood another British fort. It was the old French fort, Chambly, which had been standing in its existing form since the elder Vaudreuil had undertaken to rebuild it in 1710. It was a square, stone structure, with walls sixteen feet high and corner bastions another eight feet higher, always looking much more impressively formidable than it really was. This fort served as the main supply depot for St. Jean. After the first American incursion into Canada in May, it had been garrisoned, on Carleton's orders, by Major Stopford and six officers, five sergeants, three drummers and fifers and 62 rank and file of the 7th Regiment from Quebec, and one officer and four other ranks of the Royal Artillery. According to one writer, Fort Chambly was more in the nature of a summer hotel than a fortress, the large number of women and children sharing accomodation with their men in the fort giving colour to this statement.[25] Chambly was not, however, the kind of a fortress that could stand up to the battering that St. Jean was undergoing; but then no one ever expected that it would have to do so. Few soldiers at that time anticipated that, as long as St. Jean held out against the enemy, there was any real threat to Chambly.

Chambly was, however, located in the heart of the region in which American political propaganda had made the greatest headway. Livingston and Duggan, with Brown's help and Montgomery's blessing, had already infiltrated into this region and established a camp for Canadian enrolments at Pointe Olivier. Duggan had, in fact, succeeded in running two boats, each carrying a 9 pounder gun, down the Richelieu and past Preston's inattentive

An aquatint by Col. J. Bouchette engraved by J. & C. Walker, showing Fort Chambly as it appeared circa 1815.

sentinels on the night of September 13th, and Brown had joined him with a number of Americans whom he had marched through the woods. It is difficult, if not impossible, to determine just how many Canadians were induced to throw in their lot with Livingston and Duggan, particularly as there was a great deal of coming and going with recruits remaining for long or short periods according to their inclinations. The constant complaints of the Americans that the Canadians were never to be relied upon is evidence of this fact. Probably an estimate of two hundred Canadians would not be unfair; this at least is the number given by American sources on October 5th.[26]

It was apparently James Livingston who first advanced the idea of laying siege to Fort Chambly. And it was Livingston who carried it out, with the support of Duggan and Brown — the turncoat Hazen, convinced that the Americans represented the winning side, had also thrown in his lot with Montgomery. Livingston and Brown assembled a force estimated to be from 200 to 500 strong, threw up works and proceeded to lay siege to the fort. There was a great deal of bluff behind their preparations, for Stopford, despite the smallness of his garrison, had sufficient guns and powder to nullify anything in the way of artillery that Livingston could bring into action. But Stopford seems to have been mesmerized by the movements of his opponents and after a day and a half, in which the Americans did little damage other than to knock down one of the chimneys of the fort, he decided to surrender. There is little historical evidence about the siege and surrender of Chambly, and it is difficult at this distance to see any justification for Stopford's haste. If it was Preston's duty to defend Fort St. Jean "to the last Extremity" — and these had been Prescott's orders to the commandant at St. Jean — then it was surely Stopford's duty to do the same at Chambly. Above all, he should have realized that, in the absence of any relief for St. Jean, the safety of that fort depended upon its being held until a reluctant winter should arrive with sufficient impact to compel the Americans to withdraw into winter quarters. The honourable major is even more to be criticized for having failed, once he had resolved to surrender, to destroy his stores of provisions and ammunition, and thus to prevent them from falling into the hands of a foe who badly needed them and was greedy for them. Had he at least done this, Stopford would have yielded nothing to the Americans beyond his honour.

To the south, the officers and men of Preston's garrison listened intently as they heard the sound of guns in the direction of Chambly. What it meant, they did not know. Not, at least, for two days. Then on the 20th they found out. Two Americans appeared on the edge of the woods north of the redoubt, bearing a flag of truce. They were brought in blindfolded. With them, they carried a letter from Stopford requesting safe passage for American bateaux passing Fort St. Jean, bearing the baggage and the women and children from Chambly. Stopford and his men would march on foot.

They were prisoners of war on their way to a prison camp in New England.
Preston gave the necessary permission and on the 21st his garrison gloomily
watched the American bateaux slowly pass up-stream. Only three of the
soldiers were happy. They were the husbands of three women who had been
caught at Chambly when the siege began, and who were permitted by
Montgomery to join their spouses and friends at St. Jean.

The loss of Chambly did irreparable damage to Preston and, incidentally,
to Carleton. It dampened the enthusiasm of those Canadians who had
remained loyal to the government and convinced the less enthusiastic that
there was no point in supporting a cause which obviously had neither the
strength nor will to defend itself. It brought discouragement to Preston's
garrison which had faced hardships and short supplies with a good heart.
Several Canadian volunteers inside the fort even asked Preston's permission

to capitulate to the Americans on their own behalf, a request which met only with his angry refusal. But Preston had good cause to wonder if the contagion might not spread to others. As Stopford's miserable performance lowered the morale of the British and their Canadian adherents, so too did it bring comfort and relief to the Americans. Faced with sickness, lack of provisions, shortages of powder and ball, and the surrender of Ethan Allen, there were those Yankee faint-hearts who had been ready to call off the whole operation. Now, with their bellies and their powder horns filled, and their spirits stimulated, they changed their minds. Stopford's timidity went a long way to ensure the success of Montgomery's Montreal campaign.

There remained, however, the possibility that Carleton might still muster

St. Johns (St. Jean)

enough men and enough confidence to make an effort to relieve the beleaguered garrison at St. Jean. But Carleton was in a state of perplexity. He did not trust his militia; neither did he place much reliance on his seigneurs. He deeply resented their constant criticism of his inactivity and yet he dared not risk the little force he possessed in any major operation. He was prepared to authorize a small reconnaissance expedition, like that carried out by Captain McLeod, who crossed the St. Lawrence into Longueuil and returned with food and ammunition, and another into Boucherville, which returned with nothing at all. He was also willing to send boat patrols along the south shore opposite Montreal, provided they did not get close enough to trade shots with the enemy. In spite of the turn out of militia after the defeat of Allen and the arrest of Walker, he had been disturbed by the presence of Canadians among Allen's raiders and among those of Brown and Livingston. He was still more shaken by the fate of the Sieur de Rigauville who, while drumming up militia along the south shore, allowed himself, through his own imprudence, to be surprised and captured by a mixed force of Americans and Canadian partisans.

Finally Carleton could procrastinate no longer. The situation at St. Jean was desperate and he knew it. Something would have to be done. The governor therefore set about organizing a relief force. Instructions were sent to Colonel Allan Maclean at Quebec to add to his handful of Emigrants as many militiamen as could be induced to enlist and to move with them to Sorel and up the Richelieu towards Chambly and St. Jean. He, Carleton, would assemble a force at Montreal, cross the St. Lawrence to Longueuil and join Maclean on the Richelieu in front of St. Jean. It was a simple plan: with a little luck and more determination he might have pulled it off.

There was no shilly-shally about Maclean. The Scotsman mustered a force of 120 Royal Highland Emigrants and 60 Fusiliers at Quebec and a number of Canadian militia. At Trois Rivières, with the help of Godefroy de Tonnancour, he obtained a few more recruits, and on October 14th moved to Sorel. Here he met Captain Chabot with an armed schooner and several bateaux bearing arms and ammunition intended for the use of his brigade. At this point Maclean's success seemed to inspire a number of Canadians to join his ranks, and although he was unable to obtain any men in Nicolet, he did manage to build up a force of some 400 Canadian militia at Sorel.[27] Then, just as he was ready to begin his march towards St. Denis and Chambly, he received news from Carleton. It was not good news.

It was October 30th when Carleton finally got around to organizing his relief force in Montreal. He called upon both the Canadians and the Indians for help, although he did not venture to approach the Caughnawaga who, he suspected with good reason, had been engaged in rather dubious transactions with Montgomery's agents.[28] Despite the fact that he had really missed the opportunity to take advantage of the enthusiasm engendered by the capture of Allen and the arrest of Walker, Carleton did succeed in building up, on St.

Corporal and private soldiers of Maclean's Royal Highland Emigrants. From a drawing by Charles McBarron.

Helen's island, midway between Montreal and Longueuil, a force comprising some 800 Canadian militia, 130 Royal Highland Emigrants and Fusiliers and 80 Indians. His whole striking force was then embarked in boats and set in motion towards the south shore of the St. Lawrence late in the afternoon. It was led by Carleton himself, the Sieur St. Luc de La Corne and Lorimier. As the boats approached Longueuil they came under the fire of Americans posted along the shore by Seth Warner, Allen's former comrade in arms and later rival for command of the Green Mountain Boys. Warner had with him about 350 men and several field pieces which had been surrendered by Stopford at Chambly. Blasted by the enemy's grape and musketry, Carleton wavered. His men were willing, but a direct frontal approach was too much for undisciplined troops and the American fire threw them into confusion. His own cannon, carried in one of the boats, was unable to reply, and Carleton gave the order to withdraw. Appreciating better than their commander the advantages of an indirect approach, a few of the Canadians and Indians swung to the right, up-stream, and managed to effect a landing. But without support from Carleton their numbers were too few, and after a sharp exchange of fire in which three Conosadaga Indians were killed, the Canadians and the remaining Indians decamped. The Americans did, however, capture two miserable Canadians who were left behind, Jean Baptiste Despins and a barber by the name of Lacoste. Back on St. Helen's island Carleton's soldiers cooked themselves a meal and talked, some of them very critically, about the governor's military leadership.[29]

The failure of Carleton's ill-conducted expedition of October 30th was fatal to Maclean's hopes. The Scotsman tried to push ahead as far as St. Denis, but with his ranks depleted by desertions and opposed by a growing force of Americans led by Brown and Livingston, he was forced to pull back towards Sorel. There he dismissed what remained of his militia and with his regulars hurried off to Quebec, which was, under a jittery Cramahé, virtually defenceless.

The fiasco at Longueuil was fatal, too, to Preston. The troops at St. Jean had been ready to hold out bravely as long as they believed in the possibility of a relief force fighting its way through the American cordon to bring them help. They were, however, nearing the end of their rations and heartily sick of a steady diet of salt pork and roots; and sick too of the mud and the filth and the cold, wet weather. Sensing that the end could not be far off, the Americans increased the tempo and violence of their bombardments after the fall of Chambly. A new gun position was opened up, and although a patrol conducted by Captains Monin and McKay returned with accurate information about the location of the new battery, they also brought back word that Montgomery's force, independently of the troops under Warner, Brown and Livingston, now numbered 2000 effectives. Finally, on November 1st, the new battery opened fire. It gave Fort St. Jean the worst working over it had received since the beginning of the siege. The casualties were small in numbers but a considerable quantity of much-needed provisions was destroyed, and when Preston called for a report, he was told that at the existing rate of 2/3 rations, there was just enough food left inside the walls of the fort to feed the defenders for eight more days.

Later the same evening, after the cannonade had ceased, an American drummer beat a parley and a lone figure approached the fort. He was Lacoste, who had been taken prisoner by Warner at Longueuil. He carried a letter from Montgomery addressed to Major Preston. The letter informed Preston of the defeat of Carleton's relief force and entreated him "to spare the lives of a brave Garrison entitled to every indulgence"; it also warned the British commander that should he "obstinately persist in a defence which cannot avail," the Americans would deem themselves "innocent of the melancholy consequences which may attend. . . ."[30]

Preston sought to gain a little time by discussion. On November 2nd he sent Captain Strong, under a flag of truce, to see Montgomery. Strong argued that the Canadians in St. Jean considered Lacoste an unreliable witness, and declared that the reports Montgomery had obtained from British deserters regarding the state of the garrison's supplies and morale were inaccurate. He submitted Preston's counter proposal, namely, that the St. Jean garrison would surrender if, after four more days, the fort was not relieved. Montgomery was as aware of the importance of the time factor as Preston. He rejected Strong's proposals but allowed him to talk with Despins, the other prisoner taken at Longueuil, who confirmed all that Lacoste had said. Strong therefore returned to St. Jean with a letter containing Montgomery's rejection and threatening that if the British commander did not surrender at once, "The Garrison shall be Prisoners of War — they shall not have the honours of War — and I can not assure the Officers their baggage."[31]

Despite his desperate situation, Preston still was not ready to yield. He consulted his brother officers, and only when he found them in favour of accepting the American conditions did he agree to capitulate. Terms were then set on paper and both commanders, after some discussion, signed them on the evening of November 2nd. There was really only one sour note of disagreement; that occurred when Montgomery tried to insert words expressing his regret that the British effort at St. Jean had not been executed "in a better cause." Preston demanded the erasure of these words, asserting that his men were "determined rather to die with their arms in their Hands, than submit to the Indignity of such a Reflection."[32] Although he had the fervour of a convert, Montgomery was still soldier enough to recognize the seriousness and the reasonableness of Preston's threat to continue fighting, and the offending words were omitted in the final draft of the terms of capitulation. The next day, on November 3rd, the British troops, their drums beating and their colours flying, marched out of St. Jean with the honours of war. Stoically and gallantly they had held Fort St. Jean for fifty-five days and as a mark of his respect, Montgomery permitted the British officers to retain their swords. The troops continued to the American camp, grounded their muskets, and embarked in the water craft which were to take them on the first leg of their long journey to Connecticut. Before they left St. Jean, Preston fired one parting shot at the victors. In his journal he wrote a stinging criticism of the lack of vigour and determination with which the

Guy Carleton, Governor of Quebec (1768-1778; 1786-1796) who was the principal author of the Quebec Act and who was knighted for his successful defence of Quebec.

Americans had pushed the siege: "We may thank our Enemy in some sort for leaving us in such slight field Works the credit of having been only reduc'd by Famine. Had they understood, or been a fit people to carry on obsidional Operations, Their Batterys might with their numbers by means of Approaches have been brought much closer to our Redoubts, have overlook'd us, destroyed our breastworks, and by a slaughter from which there cou'd have been no Shelter, have render'd our holding out, a meer sacrifice of Men who might have been reserv'd for better Services."[33]

During the siege the defenders had suffered forty-three casualties, twenty of which were fatal. Of these, the Indians and the Canadians accounted for almost half. There were twenty-three wounded, of which by far the greater number were regulars. The Americans suffered no more than one hundred casualties in all. The distress from disease had been much greater. As early as October 12th, no less than 937 Americans had been discharged as unfit for further duty, and Montgomery thought seriously of resigning his command.

But now the American commander harboured no such defeatist thoughts. The way was open to him to march to Montreal and he set out almost immediately. It was important for him not to delay his movements, for Arnold had been, by this time, six weeks on the journey to Quebec. At the same time he saw the advantages of blocking any troop withdrawal from Montreal, and ordered Colonel James Easton's corps along with Brown and Livingston to hurry forward to Sorel. Their object was to establish themselves on the south shore of the St. Lawrence, and, if the opportunity offered itself, on the north as well.

IV. The Surrender of Montreal

Carleton was in a state of despair on November 4th when he learned of the capitulation of St. Jean. He wrote at once to Dartmouth sending him the doleful news and placing the blame, not upon himself, but upon the failure of the military and naval authorities at Halifax to send him the necessary shipwrights and artificers to construct the vessels he needed to control Lake Champlain, upon the ill-disposition of the Canadian population, and upon "those Traytors within, who by their Art and insinuation are still more dangerous to the publick safety." Now, all that remained to him would be to salvage whatever he could from the stores at Montreal and embark the garrison and all available guns and ammunition and provisions on the vessels in the harbour and set out for Quebec, where, he told Dartmouth, "The prospect . . . is not much better; Accounts say B. Arnold is on the Chaudière, with twelve or fifteen hundred Men, we have not one Soldier in the Town, & the lower sort are not much more loyal than here."[34] Why Carleton did not sail at once can only be surmised; perhaps he regarded it as a point of honour to remain in Montreal until the American troops had actually crossed the river and were on the threshold of the city. He procrastinated almost to the end.

Pierre-Meru Panet, a notary who was one of the citizens of Montreal who negotiated the surrender of the city to Montgomery, and who later served as a member of Carleton's commission which examined the role of collaborators in Montreal during the American invasion.

In the meantime the citizens of Montreal prepared to receive the invaders. Those elements of the population who had favoured the rebel cause, and those who were now prepared to make the best of a bad thing, met and drafted the terms on which they would agree to surrender the town. At the same time Montgomery sent three men to talk to the people of Montreal. One of them was James Price, the former Montrealer, who was acting as adviser as well as banker to Montgomery. According to Sanguinet, Price was less disposed than the American commander to be lenient to his former townsmen; but in the end articles of capitulation were agreed upon which were signed on behalf of the people of Montreal by John Porteous, Pierre Panet, John Blake, Pierre Mezière, James Finlay, St. George Dupré, James McGill, Louis Carignan, Richard Huntly, François Malhiot, Edward W. Gray and Pierre Guy. Montgomery treated the terms laid before him in a summary fashion. After all, he did not have to negotiate with anybody for Montreal. He knew that the town was in no position to defend itself, that its walls were weak and its people lacking martial zeal, that it possessed few guns or men to man them, that it was short of provisions and short of ammunition. Knowing this, however, he was willing to be magnanimous. He would not argue with the citizens of Montreal, he came as their friend "for the express purpose" of bringing them "liberty and security"; he would leave everybody in Montreal to "the peaceable enjoyment of their property, of every kind."[35] At 9 o'clock on November 13th the American troops formally entered the Recollet gate. They received the keys of the public storehouses and then marched to the barracks so recently vacated by Carleton's men.

The pro-American group was jubilant. No longer would they have to hold their tongues. Forty of them, therefore, drew up and presented to Montgomery an address of welcome. In it they called his attention to their claims as the only true and sincere friends of Congress; they stressed their anxiety to join the American union, and warned Montgomery against listening to those other Montrealers who had supported Carleton and treated the followers of Congress as rebels. No consideration should be given to them; they were Tories who should be treated as a "conquered people."[36]

Montgomery did not choose to remain at Montreal, despite the lateness of the year and the onset of the first snows of winter. Chambly, St. Jean and Montreal had fallen to his troops but Quebec still remained the rock upon which British power rested in North America. Canada could not be brought into the American union, as Samuel Adams had advocated, until the redcoats had been driven from the great fortress on the St. Lawrence. Therefore the American general, after receiving the surrender of Trois Rivières, placed Brigadier General David Wooster in charge of Montreal, gave Livingston a colonel's commission and authority to raise a regiment of Canadians, made arrangements with Christophe Pélissier, the proprietor of the Forges St. Maurice, for the manufacture of guns and ammunition, and set sail for

A private of an American line regiment during the American Revolutionary War, drawn by George C. Woodbridge.

Quebec at the end of November. But the army which followed him was not the army which had brought him his victories in October and November. Most of those men had been short-service personnel, many of whom had been induced to enlist by the bogey of a British and Canadian invasion of their native land; now that the bloodybacks and the papists had been beaten, what further reason was there for them to keep on fighting? No reason sufficient to convince them to extend the legal term of their enlistment. Moreover the weather had turned a bone-chilling cold and they were not equipped for a winter campaign. As early as November 17th Montgomery was writing to Schuyler of difficulties with his troops and the determination of many of them to return to the colonies. He exhorted and he cajoled; he even borrowed £5000 from James Price for woollens with which to equip his

American militiamen as seen by a German observer at the time of the Revolutionary War.

men in warm clothing; but the majority of the New Englanders, with the exception of a few Connecticut men who remained with Wooster, turned their faces towards the south, leaving only 800 men in Montreal. And out of these, Montgomery had to provide a garrison to maintain Wooster in safety in Montreal watching the local malcontents and keeping his eye on whatever small British garrisons still remained intact on the upper St. Lawrence and the Great Lakes. When finally, on December 3rd, Montgomery reached Pointe aux Trembles (Neuville) eighteen or so miles above Quebec, he had with him, according to Benedict Arnold, no more than 300 men and a few gunners.[37] Among them were some of the New Yorkers who had panicked in the woods in the early days of the siege of St. Jean, Livingston and Duggan and a few Canadian partisans, and Major Brown with the remnants of Easton's corps at Sorel. The New Englanders and the Green Mountain Boys were conspicuous by their absence.

It was late in the afternoon of November 11th when Carleton, Prescott, the regulars of the Montreal garrison, and the prisoner, Thomas Walker, embarked in *Gaspé* and the other vessels waiting at Montreal to convey them to Quebec. A few loyal citizens saw them off at the dock. According to Sanguinet the occasion had all the atmosphere of a funeral. Carleton had finished his task. He had lost Montreal but he had left the Americans very little. He had spiked the guns of the town and destroyed or removed everything which might be of service to the enemy. Prescott had proposed to burn the barracks, but Carleton yielded to the request from some Montreal citizens that no fires should be started lest they get out of hand and lead to a general conflagration. A few last minute instructions had also been despatched to Henry Hamilton in the west, telling him to keep the king's

Montreal as Montgomery would have seen it from the south shore. The inadequacy of the city wall as a defence work is obvious. Mount Royal is in the background.

ships on the Great Lakes in good repair and to be on the alert against the day when action might be resumed against the Americans.

The wind was fair and for the first few hours Carleton's flotilla of ships and bateaux made good progress. Then, near Lavaltrie, on the 12th, one of them ran aground. By the time the fleet was ready to move again the wind began to drop and the vessels had, of necessity, to heave-to under anchor not far from Sorel. Here they remained for several days. On the 15th, to Carleton's complete surprise, a flag of truce appeared. It had never entered his head that Montgomery might split his force and that Americans might be in the vicinity. The flag of truce covered a letter demanding his surrender together with that of his ships, men and all their supplies. "If you will Resign your Fleet to me Immediately without destroying the Effects on Board," the letter read, "You and Your men shall be used with due civility together with women & Children on Board — to this I expect Your direct and Immediate answer. Should you Neglect You will Cherefully take the Consequences which will follow."[38] The governor did not take kindly to a summary demand of this kind, but he could not afford an outright rejection and so began to temporize. To convince him that the letter, which had been signed by Colonel Easton, had force behind it, Major Brown visited the British ships and offered to show any British officers his new heavy gun emplacements which could blow all of Carleton's ships out of the water if the governor refused to yield with grace. An officer was therefore appointed to examine the American emplacements; but it does not appear that he really did so. From all we can gather, it seems that he was either intimidated or hoaxed by

Charles Tarieu de Lanaudière, one of the French Canadian seigneurs who supported the British. Lanaudière served as Carleton's aide-de-camp during the invasion.

Brown's bold front; in any event he was impressed with Brown's confident assurance of the existence of a "grand battery of 32 pounder guns" and an airy wave of the hand in the general direction of Sorel. The whole story is not known. What we do know is that when Charles Carroll, an agent appointed by Congress to visit Canada, examined the defences at Sorel a few weeks later, he wrote about Brown in his diary, "His grand battery was as badly provided with cannon as his little battery, for not a single gun was mounted on either."[39]

The decision Carleton had now to make was whether the cost of damage and probable loss of life was too high to make an attempt to run the blockade which he had been led to believe existed. After all he was not helpless. His own ships of war carried thirty guns and the whole fleet would present a moving target difficult to hit for gunners who had not attained even a high level of mediocrity. But then what might be the consequences should a lucky hot shot hit the vessel carrying the gun powder? Carleton would not take it upon himself to decide and called a council of war. One of the ship captains, Belette, offered to take on the batteries and provide fire-cover for the others while they made a run for it; another, Jean Baptiste Bouchette, offered to take Carleton aboard a small boat and row him past the American position in the dark. Everybody agreed that it was essential that the governor should get to Quebec. His presence there would give inspiration to the defenders and upon the successful defence of the capital depended the fate of Canada. Carleton agreed to Bouchette's proposal — the

French Canadian's nickname, *La Tourtre*, the wild pigeon, was indicative of the speed with which he sailed his vessels, and speed was the one thing necessary if he were to reach Quebec in safety.[40] At dead of night, and clad in a woollen cap and coat, tied in at the waist with a *ceinture fléchée* in the habitant style, Carleton slipped over the side of the vessel and into Bouchette's whale boat. The oars were muffled, but as the boat passed near the shore the oarsmen put them aside and propelled their craft with their bare hands. They made no sound, and heard none from the shore. On Lake St. Pierre they were able to take to the oars again and row with vigour. On the afternoon of the 17th they reached Trois Rivières, where Carleton went ashore with his principal aide, Charles-François Tarieu de La Naudière, accompanied by the Chevalier de Niverville and Captain Bouchette. With the help of the wild pigeon, he had escaped the Yankee marksmen.

Before going over the side of *Gaspé* Carleton had given orders that all cannon, powder and ball should be dumped into the waters of the St. Lawrence before any capitulation. Then, when there was nothing left, Prescott was left free to surrender if he could not avoid it. As soon as Carleton was safely out of sight, Prescott re-examined his situation. He tried to bargain with Easton for safe passage to Quebec but Easton would have nothing of it; the British were going to have to surrender. On November 19th Prescott gave up without ever firing a shot. The British soldiers and seamen were a sad looking crew when they returned to Montreal. But one man was jubilant; he was Thomas Walker, who looked forward with pleasurable anticipation to paying off a few old scores and taking the position which he felt now would be his in Montreal under the rule of the alien David Wooster. What Montgomery thought of the whole miserable episode is contained in his letter to his wife, written on the 24th: "The other day General Prescott was so obliging as to surrender himself and fourteen or fifteen land officers, with above one hundred men, besides sea officers and sailors, prisoners of war! I blushed for His Majesty's troops! such an instance of base poltroonery I have never met with, and all because we had half a dozen cannon on the bank of the river to annoy him in his retreat! The Governor escaped — more's the pity. Prescott, nevertheless, is a prize."[41] Montgomery got even more than the prisoners he mentioned in his letter. Prescott had not thrown everything overboard, and the Americans happily seized the ships' cannon, a stand of small arms, and two hundred pairs of shoes! What was even more fortunate from Montgomery's point of view was that by this unexpected windfall he acquired the vessels he needed to transport himself and his men down the St. Lawrence to Quebec to join Benedict Arnold.

Although Carleton had reached Trois Rivières in safety, he was still not out of danger. He was assured there were no Americans in the town, but was warned that some of Arnold's men were at Pointe aux Trembles, between Trois Rivières and Quebec. Carleton could scarcely credit it, but there was confirmation from reliable sources, including Tonnancour. No time was to be lost. The governor and La Naudière therefore embarked again and set off down stream. Fortunately they fell in with the British snow, *Fell*, which sailed with all possible speed to Quebec encountering no opposition as it passed Pointe aux Trembles. On Sunday, November 19th, the vessel arrived at Quebec and Carleton climbed the steep hill from the dock to the Chateau of St. Louis. Thomas Ainslie called it "A happy day for Quebec," and recorded in his diary, "to the unspeakable joy of the friends of Government, & to the utter dismay of the abettors of sedition & rebellion: Gen: Carleton arrived in the *Fell*, arm'd ship, accompanied by an arm'd schooner — we saw our salvation in his presence."[42] Carleton himself was not so sure about the salvation. Reporting the events of the past week to Dartmouth he was only cautiously optimistic, "Could the People in the Town, and Seamen, be depended upon, I should flatter myself, we might hold out, till the Navigation opens next Spring, at least till a few Troops might come up the River, for I fear the Delays commonly attending a large armament; but tho' the severe weather is far advanced, we have so many Enemies within, and foolish People. Dupes to those Traitors, with the natural Fears of Men unused to war, I think our Fate extremely doubtful, to say nothing worse."[43]

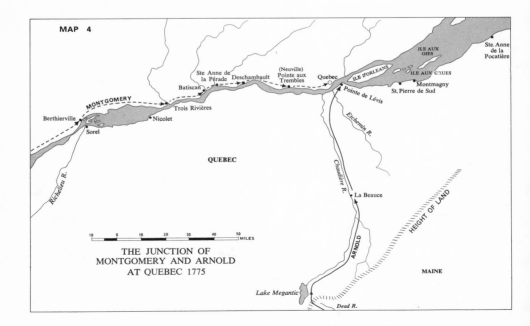

MAP 4

THE JUNCTION OF
MONTGOMERY AND ARNOLD
AT QUEBEC 1775

III The Quebec Campaign 1775-1776

I. Benedict Arnold's March to Quebec

The right wing of the American invasion force mustered initially in Cambridge, Massachusetts, in September 1775, marched to Newburyport, and then embarked in sea transport which took it to the mouth of the Kennebec River. The sea passage was not a smooth one, but then very little in this expedition went smoothly. However, the troops reached their destination at Gardiner's Town and then pushed on to Fort Western, now Augusta, Maine, some forty miles or more up river from the sea. All told the eastern division numbered about 1200 men, of whom a considerable number were riflemen from Virginia and Pennsylvania, armed men of a kind which had not been included in Montgomery's force. The remainder were ordinary infanteers from the several New England colonies. All of them were rude, hardy, fearless men, speaking with different accents but all sharing an aversion to military discipline and firmly believing that they were fighting for God and liberty. John Henry, who was one of them in 1775, was fascinated by the arms and costumes of the Virginians and Pennsylvanians. Each rifleman, he wrote in his account, carried "a rifle-barreled gun, a tomahawk, or small axe, and a long knife, usually called a "scalping knife," which served for all purposes in the woods"; he wore an "under-dress, by no means in a military style . . . covered by a deep ash-colored hunting shirt, leggins, and moccasins." To Henry it was "the silly fashion of those times for riflemen to ape the manners of savages"[1] even if to Washington it was cheap, sensible and convenient. The driving power behind this motley group of soldiers was their commanding officer, Benedict Arnold, a man possessing a greater capacity to inspire than to organize an expedition of the type he was about to undertake. Short, stout and of florid complexion, he was brave to temerity and was admired by his men, "perhaps for this quality only," said Henry. A strange compound of opposites, Arnold was one of the most remarkable non-professional, natural military leaders in American history.

71

At Fort Western the army was organized in four divisions. The first included Daniel Morgan's riflemen, the second and third the infantry companies under Christopher Greene and Jonathan Return Meigs, and the fourth or rear guard, under Roger Enos. It was in this order that Arnold's army began its ascent of the Kennebec in large flat-bottomed bateaux. These water craft had been built by special contract in less than three weeks; they were made of freshly-sawn, green lumber. Arnold was not very happy with them. "Many of them smaller than the directions given, and badly, very badly built," he wrote to Washington.[2] Each bateau carried a cargo of kegs and barrels, and was poled upstream by its sweating crew, the soldiers marching along the shore to lend a hand whenever necessary. Arnold's expedition was not striking off into the unknown. The details of Montresor's journal and maps were known to Arnold and to Washington, and the American commander had taken the precaution of sending scouts in advance to keep him informed of the obstacles he might expect to encounter. It was September 25th when Morgan's division led off with orders to proceed to the Great Carrying Place and to cut a road over the height of land. Each division followed in turn on successive days. The auguries were fair; even the weather smiled upon the poling and marching men. Only one unfortunate incident occurred to mar the occasion, and even this Arnold felt could be turned to a useful purpose. One of the soldiers murdered a comrade; he was tried by court martial and condemned to hang. The sentence was not, however, carried out; the man was paraded with a halter around his neck so that the troops might take note of what military discipline could mean in time of war, and then sent home for Washington's disposal. It was a healthy lesson, for bad blood among men could cripple any fighting force.

By October 2nd Arnold, who had waited to see all his divisions under way, reached the falls at Norridgewock, travelling quickly in a dugout canoe. So far his men had been moving through inhabited country; now they were about to enter the wilderness. At Norridgewock Arnold watched Morgan's corps as they manhandled their heavy bateaux over the long portage, and he was not pleased with what he saw. Despite the fact that the expedition had been only ten days on the move, the bateaux had been severely battered and in some instances broken. Even more suggestive of future problems was the condition of the rations. Isaac Senter, a young medical student who had left his studies to enlist in the Rhode Island contingent as a medical officer, tells in his journal that he saw dried codfish "lying loose in the batteaux and being continually washed with the fresh water running into the batteaux." The bread casks had turned to soggy dough; not being waterproof, they "admitted the water in plenty, swelled the bread, burst the casks, as well as soured the bread." These and several casks of peas Senter was obliged to condemn, despite the fact that it meant looking forward to a none too appetising diet of salt pork and flour with only the occasional piece of beef. But the beef was of "so indifferent quality" as to be scarcely fit to eat,

Arnold's expedition across the wilderness — boat on wheels.

"being killed in the heat of summer." Moreover, it had become damaged after salting which "rendered it not only very unwholesome, but very unpalatable."[3] It may have been the army contractor who was to blame for shoddy workmanship on the bateaux and the barrels — at least some of the troops thought so — but Arnold felt a portion, at least, of the responsibility for the breakages had to rest with the inexperienced bateaumen he had been compelled to employ.

The carpenters set to work at once and the damaged bateaux were soon ready to be on the way again. Arnold was not a leader who was tolerant of delay. There were many rapids and portages yet to be passed and the days were beginning to get colder and wetter. On the 11th Arnold reached the Great Carrying Place, a location which elicited favourable comment on the "beautiful prospect"[4] from Captain Simeon Thayer, but which brought forth only oaths and curses from the men who had to struggle leg-deep in the morass to get their bateaux over the wet, swampy ground. Here was the entrance to the Dead River, an ominous name to those wretched beings suffering from the physical strain of hard labour and from rations they could not stomach. The drinking water, in particular, was "of the worst quality." It was obviously polluted — Senter said that it was "quite yellow." And with a diet of salt pork combined with heavy work, the men were inclined to drink great quantities. The results were not fatal, but distinctly unpleasant; in some instances, diarrhoea, in others, vomiting. Senter wrote, "No sooner had it got down than it was puked up by many of the poor fellows."[5] In order better to look after the increasing number of casualties, some of which were becoming serious, Senter urged that a building should be erected "for the reception of our sick." Arnold agreed, and a log cabin was constructed to which Senter gave the name of Arnold's Hospital. But the young medical officer did not remain behind to minister to the patients who filled his little hospital; Arnold demanded as much of his men as he demanded of himself, and when the troops moved on, Senter went with them. The most serious cases were therefore left behind in their discomfort, their vomit and their vermin.

Arnold, with his thoughts always directed towards Quebec, spent a few moments at the Great Carrying Place writing letters. One he sent to Washington to inform the commander in chief that "the greatest difficulty" was "already past" and that he expected to reach the Chaudière River in eight or ten days;[6] the second was addressed to General Schuyler, asking for "intelligence or advice";[7] and the third, to John Dyer Mercier, a pro-American collaborator living inside the walls of Quebec. To this last, Arnold wrote announcing his impending arrival "with about 2000 men," a slight exaggeration excusable under the circumstances, and revealing the fact that his force was "designed to co-operate with General Schuyler to frustrate the unjust and arbitrary mesures of the Ministry and restore Liberty to our Brethren of Canada, to whom we made no doubt that our exertions in their favour will be acceptable." He then urged Mercier to send word about "the Disposition of the Canadians, the number of Troops in Quebec, by whom commanded . . . what ships are at Quebec, and in short what we have to expect from the Canadians and Merchants in the City." He asked Mercier to get this information to him as soon as possible by messenger, who would be "received with pleasure and handsomely rewarded."[8] It was an injudicious, even dangerous, letter, but Arnold needed information and was prepared to

Arnold's journey through the wilderness. Polling a boat.

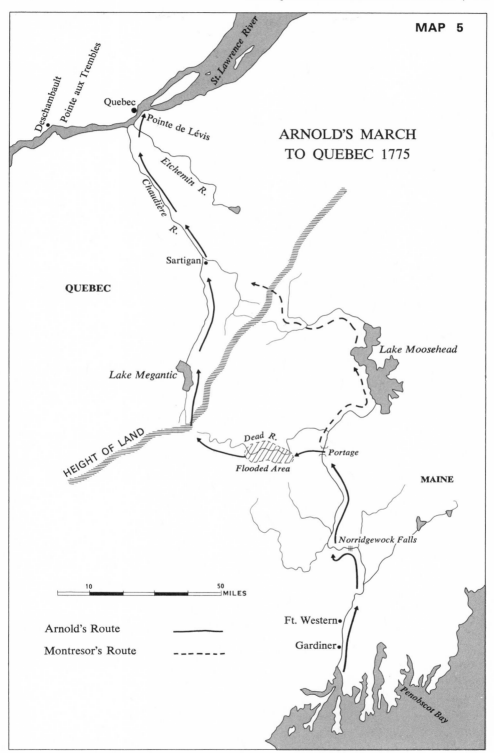

MAP 5

ARNOLD'S MARCH
TO QUEBEC 1775

St. Lawrence River

Deschambault

Pointe aux Trembles

Quebec

Pointe de Lévis

Etchemin R.

Chaudière R.

Sartigan

QUEBEC

Lake Megantic

Lake Moosehead

HEIGHT OF LAND

Dead R.

Portage

Flooded Area

MAINE

Norridgewock Falls

Ft. Western

Gardiner

Penobscot Bay

10   50
⊢MILES

Arnold's Route ——————

Montresor's Route - - - - - - -

run the risk of having his letters intercepted. Neither the Schuyler nor the Mercier letter ever reached its destination. The Indian runner who carried them, by mistake or by design, turned both letters over to the British authorities, and the secrets of Arnold's march and the name of his principal contact in the city were then revealed to the government at Quebec.

The journey up the Dead River to the height of land offered Arnold's men their greatest challenge. Poor, weary men, they struggled over the frequent portages, through the cedar swamps, and over the miry roads; but the heavy winds and the everlasting rain that made placid rivulets into rushing torrents, the river banks that "became prodigiously mountainous, closing as it were up the river with an aspect of immense height," the confusing networks of lakes and tributaries, imposed new hazards upon an army seriously concerned about its growing food shortage and weak, inadequate transportation. Already there was a steady stream of invalids making their way slowly back towards the civilization they wished they had never left. In the early hours of October 22nd Arnold was awakened by a wall of water which descended upon the camp, the river "having rose 8 feet perpendicular in 9 hours, and before we could remove, wet all our Baggage."[9] The commander and his men took refuge on a nearby hill, and then gazed at the melancholy prospect before them, a river overflowed and a valley flooded. Who was to tell where the main current was to be found, or determine the route to be followed?

Then there were problems of morale more serious even than those of a physical nature. On the 25th a council of war was held. Colonel Enos acted as chairman. The army was divided on the course of action it should follow. The "melancholy aspects who had been preaching to their men the doctrine of impenetrability and non-perseverance,"[10] as Dr. Senter called them, were ready to abandon the whole enterprise. Others, inspired by Arnold's determination and conviction of success, were ready to continue. As far as Arnold was concerned he never, at any time, contemplated giving up. To him this was the course of weakness, fit only for the sick and the timorous. Duty and honour demanded his advance. Each commander was, therefore, told to weed out the weaklings, give them several bateaux and send them back to the coast. The rest, the fittest, were to go on, carrying with them fifteen days' provisions. But Colonel Enos's men of the rear guard would have none of this. They had manhandled more than their share, or so they felt, and kept the supplies moving up to satisfy the forward troops. Now there were not many barrels of provisions left, and they had no intention of parting with them. Neither did they have any intention of continuing to struggle through a land that would soon be buried deep in snow. Enos had completely lost control of his men and Arnold found himself facing what amounted to a mutiny. There was not much he could do about it, and when Enos's men finally agreed to turn over to the rest of the army a miserable pittance of no more than two and a half barrels of flour and return southward, taking Enos with them, Arnold let them go. "Captain Williams stept'd towards me, and wish'd me success," wrote Simeon Thayer, "But in the meantime told me he never expected to see me, or any of us, he was so conscious of the imminent Danger we were to go through."[11] But the men in the ranks did not exchange polite farewells with their comrades in Colonel Enos's division. Those of Captain Dearborn's company were probably no different from those in the other companies which elected to remain with Arnold; according to their company commander they "made a General Prayer, that Colo: Enos and all his men, might die by the way, or meet with some disaster Equal to the Cowardly dastardly and unfriendly Spirit they discover'd in returning Back without Orders, in such a manner as they had done. And then we proceeded forward," he added.[12]

Reduced now to about 800 men, Arnold's army shoved blindly on.

Arnold's men at the portage at the Norridgewock Falls, on the Kennebec river.

Among the woods, over the rocks, through a series of small lakes and up the height of land they waded and toiled, weakened by hunger and chilled by the cold. Boats upset and men were drowned; others simply collapsed from sheer exhaustion and fatigue. The lack of adequate and sufficient rations was what plagued them most. On November 1st Captain William Goodrich's men killed Dearborn's dog and ate it. John Henry's comrades washed their moosehide moccasins, scraped away the dirt and sand, and boiled them. Henry did not find the result very satisfactory; "the poor fellows chewed the leather; but it was leather still, not to be macerated. My teeth, though young and good, succeeded no better."[13] Dr. Senter fared almost as badly. On October 27th he noted in his journal, "Our bill of fare for last night and this morning consisted of the jawbone of a swine destitute of any covering. This we boiled in a quantity of water, that with a little thickening constituted our sumptuous eating."[14] Yet few wanted to turn back to retrace their steps and follow in the wake of the·disillusioned and disgraced men of Colonel Enos's

A view of Quebec by Captain Hervey Smyth, showing the city as it would have appeared to Arnold's men on the south shore.

corps, even when they had to trudge on foot, having abandoned most of their ponderous boats. In the end they won through. Once over the height of land they could see Lake Mégantic in the distance and from it they knew the Chaudière flowed directly to the St. Lawrence. By October 30th, Arnold, who was in the van, succeeded in reaching the first Canadian settlement, Sartigan, on the Chaudière. Here he was received with hospitality, and arrangements were made to send back to the struggling column the supplies they so badly needed. By November 4th most of Arnold's gaunt, emaciated, verminous men had reached the settled region; only a few stragglers and the dead remained behind in the desolation of hills and valleys through which the others had passed. Finally, on November 8th American troops reached Pointe de Lévis about an hour or two after midnight. It was snowing.

The following day the invaders could see the great stone bulk that was Quebec on the opposite side of the St. Lawrence. They still had to make their way across the river and the British had taken the precaution of removing all the canoes from the south shore and the Island of Orleans. But the omens were good. A young midshipman, from the sloop of war, *Hunter*, was captured while reconnoitring the vicinity of Pointe de Lévis; the Americans had thus drawn the first blood. Arnold himself was jubilant. He wrote to both Montgomery and Mercier, telling the first of his arrival on the St. Lawrence and informing the other that "if possible" he would cross the river in two or three days, and "if practicable" would assault the fortress of Quebec. His first statement he made good on the night of November 15th. Obtaining some canoes from nearby Indians, he slipped quietly over the river under cover of the darkness, evading detection from the hourly British patrols on the river. Once on shore he seized Colonel Henry Caldwell's house at Ste. Foye, which he made his headquarters, and sent his men to occupy the nearby farm buildings. There was no sign of action in Quebec and the

Americans, dead tired, tried to snatch what sleep they could. So too did one of Arnold's sentinels, a young man from Morgan's corps, who found himself in the hands of a British reconnaissance patrol, "even before he had time to cock his rifle."[15] Suddenly the Americans were awakened by shouts that the British were upon them. Anticipating a sortie from the fortress, Arnold mustered his tatterdemalion host, all 500 of them, and when no British troops appeared, marched them boldly "in front and opposite to the wall of the city" before "hundreds of gaping citizens and soldiers" standing on the walls of Quebec.[16] The Americans shook the air with three mighty huzzas, but Quebec was no Jericho and a reply came in the form of a round of grape and canister from several of the cannons on the wall. Arnold's audacious act of defiance may have been the kind of thing that appealed to most Americans, but one of them, John Henry, regarded it as "farcical" — so also did Morgan and other officers, if we can believe Henry's account. Henry clearly did not like Arnold and felt that his demonstration had been motivated simply by a sense of vanity and a desire to display his power to the British who had so frequently referred to him by the slighting epithet of "horse jockey."

For six days Colonel Arnold and his men remained inactive in front of Quebec. The American commander's attempts to get his bombastic demand for the surrender of the fortress into the hands of the British authorities were thwarted when the gates of the city remained locked to his flags of truce. Not only that, his messengers had been warned away by a musket ball or two sent in their direction. As far as his talk of assaulting the fortress was concerned, that had been merely for the sake of maintaining the morale of his troops. He knew that he had neither the men nor the arms to do it. The whole idea was as preposterous as it was impracticable. All that Arnold could do for the moment was to send out occasional forage parties to pick up rations and to write letters of protest to Cramahé complaining of the manner in which his flags of truce had been abused. On November 16th a forage

Colonel Allan Maclean of Torloisk who raised The Royal Highland Emigrants and played a decisive role in the defence of Canada during the American invasion of 1775-1776. From a miniature at Duart Castle.

party managed to drive in a few cattle; but the loss of a sergeant, whose leg was severed by a cannon ball, seemed to be a very high price for several yearlings and an old cow. The sergeant, Dixon by name, at least immortalized himself in the history of his country by refusing a bowl of tea offered him to ease his suffering, in the words, "No madam, it is the ruin of my country."[17] The fact is that, despite his assumed attitude of complete confidence, Arnold was worried. Far too many of the cartridges his men had lugged over the Kennebec and the height of land had been damaged and too much of his gunpowder had been rendered useless by water. A considerable number of his muskets, too, were so badly battered as to be beyond repair. In a candid letter to Montgomery, Arnold stated that he possessed no more than five rounds per man; "Add to this many of the men invalids," he wrote, "and almost naked and wanting every thing to make them comfortable."[18]

His spies in Quebec had surprised him with reports of the unexpected strength of the garrison, and believing that Colonel Maclean might take advantage of this superiority of numbers to try an attack, Arnold decided to withdraw beyond reach of Maclean's troops by moving up the St. Lawrence towards Montreal and General Montgomery's army. This movement was carried out on November 18th, according to one of the participants "in a slovenly style, accompanied, probably, by the maledictions of the clergy and nobility, but attended by the regrets of a host of well-wishers among the peasantry."[19]

While marching along the north shore road in the direction of Pointe aux Trembles, John Henry observed "the rapid passage, down stream, of a boat, and soon afterwards of a ship." What Henry did not know was that the ship he saw was H. M. S. *Fell*, and that it was bearing the governor of Canada, Guy Carleton, and his aide to Quebec.

II. Carleton's Preparations for the Defence of Quebec

From inside the walls, Quebec did not present the same impression of formidable strength as it did from outside. As in Montreal, there were divided counsels, particularly among the English-speaking population. The English merchants, like their counterparts in Montreal, had agitated for the establishment of an elected assembly. John McCord and Zachary Macaulay had both been prominent when the demand for an assembly had been advanced in 1773, and both had joined forces with Walker and Price to demonstrate against the Quebec Act. When the troubles began to boil over in Boston, they showed their solidarity with their American friends and relations, and gave practical evidence of their hostility to Gage by sending a free gift of 1000 bushels of wheat to the rebels of Boston. Then, when a letter of gratitude came from the Boston Committee of Donations together with a bundle of revolutionary propaganda leaflets, they circulated both among the inhabitants of the city and its environs. There were no open demonstrations in Quebec on May 1st, 1775 when the "abominable Act" came into effect, as there had been in Montreal — Quebec was more directly aware of the presence of the government and its authority and lacked the long tradition of violence associated with the frontier fur trading post of Montreal — but the contagion of sedition was still there poisoning the heart of the city's loyalty. Despite the fact that, late in June 1775, a few English merchants took active steps to offer their services "in protecting the King's Magazines, as well as our own Property,"[20] when an attempt was made to establish a militia, only a handful actually turned out for duty.

The appointment of General Schuyler to a military command and the obvious intention on the part of Congress to send an invading army into Canada brought about a change of attitude. It forced the English merchants of Quebec, as it did those of Montreal, to declare themselves. Many, indeed most of those who had taken an active part in the agitation against the

Quebec Act and who had encouraged the French Canadians to resist the actions of the British government, were reluctant to take the final step and shoulder their muskets against their king. Thomas Ainslie was telling the truth when he wrote in his diary that "Some of these Grumbletonians . . . see with pain that their malice has contributed to incline the Canadians to throw off their allegiance – they mean to stir them up to a General application for repeal of the Act – not to Rebellion."[21] This may explain why those who would not turn out for the militia in July, were prompt enough to answer Carleton's appeal in September. The *Quebec Gazette* reported on the 21st of that month that on the 16th, seventeen companies of militia, eleven French Canadian and six British, had mustered on the Parade in Quebec and had been reviewed by the lieutenant governor, Hector Cramahé. Two companies had subsequently been given responsibility for mounting guard. There was no protest against this action; neither was there any protest when Cramahé issued an order requiring "all Persons not settled Inhabitants of this Place who since the Thirty-first day of August have, or who hereafter shall come into the Town of Quebec, either to repair themselves immediately, or to signify to one of the Conservators of the Peace . . . their Names and place of abode, together with the occasion of their coming into the Town, upon pain of being considered and treated as Spies if they remain therein for the space of two hours without repairing themselves or giving notice as aforesaid."[22]

Meanwhile Cramahé had taken positive defence measures. He had set carpenters to work cutting and preparing pickets, in laying platforms for cannon and in repairing the blockhouses and sally ports. Several days later he had ordered the gates of the city to be locked at 9 o'clock. Five transports sent from Boston to Quebec to obtain forage were ordered not to leave the harbour and several private vessels were requisitioned by the government. To find the crews for his warships, the lieutenant governor had recourse to an embargo upon all civilian shipping tied up at Quebec. This freed a number of sailors and on October 5th the *Quebec Gazette* reported that the armed snow, *Fell*, "compleatly equipp'd with 16 nine-pounders, besides Swivels, etc., and 100 true tars, on board of which Commodore Napier hoisted his flag, hauled out into the Stream, and is now moored before this City." Several other vessels were also fitted out and placed under the command of Captains Littlejohn, Chabot and Lizotte. In the face of this demonstration of energy a number of the English-speaking residents of the city agreed publicly to defend "their lives and Properties" against the enemy "to the utmost" of their power. Cramahé accepted this for what it was worth, and then, feeling reasonably sure of himself, he took steps to arrest John Dyer Mercier, as soon as the latter's duplicity became apparent by the capture of his treasonable correspondence with Benedict Arnold.

Despite these measures, Cramahé was not a bold or fearless man. He had entered Quebec with Wolfe's army and had remained as Murray's secretary because of his French background. He was not a warrior; rather was he a timid man, an administrator whose best work was done at his desk, not a leader or an inspirer of other men. He was as much shaken as he was annoyed when some of the English merchants demanded an explanation for Mercier's arrest and detention on board one of the sloops of war in the harbour. Cramahé produced the evidence of Mercier's duplicity but wondered if some of those who were so concerned about Mercier were not of doubtful loyalty themselves. He, Cramahé, knew too, as Ainslie knew, that even though they had signed the declaration of their willingness to fight, some members of the English-speaking community were not really to be trusted, and that behind closed doors they were muttering counsels of despair. And not merely muttering, as they read reports of Montgomery's progress down the Richelieu. In his diary Ainslie wrote critically of the "anarchial method of calling town meetings" at which "ungarded speeches betray'd principles which policy had made them hide. Reports of Mr. Montgomery's successes were most industriously spread — the enemies of Government continued to watch every favourable opportunity to work on the minds of such of the Old and New subjects as seem'd not yet to be confirmed in their principles."[23] As soon as the news reached Quebec of the approach of Benedict Arnold with another American army, the pro-American sympathisers not only began openly to urge the advantages of neutrality, but even drafted articles of surrender which they felt should be put before the populace and presented to Arnold. François Baby, one of Carleton's appointees to the Legislative Council, a strong loyalist, expressed his conviction that only about half of the population in the city were to be relied upon. Far too many were inclined to shirk their guard duty. Cramahé admitted as much when he wrote despairingly to Dartmouth that the militia were "with Difficulty brought to Mount Guard and consequently not much to be depended on."[24] Even more revealing of the depth of Cramahé's concern is a letter written from Quebec early in November by one of the English residents: "Just now an order is come down for eight men from each of the six companies of the British Militia to appear on parade *without Arms*, to receive One Shilling and pint of Porter for the business they were to do. Orders are also given for a party of Marines to be on the parade *armed*. So we are inclined to judge the intentions of our Government to be to force us to a defence of the town, and sacrifice our lives and properties. The Shilling and a pint of Porter are supposed to be considered as King's money to enlist us, and subject us to military discipline. The Lord protect us from our enemies within and without."[25] The man who wrote those words was unlikely to put up much of a fight if he could save himself and his belongings by surrender. Is it surprising that Cramahé lost his temper and shouted at Zachary Macaulay, that his "damn'd committees" had thrown the province "into its present state"? When his anger had subsided, he wrote in great gloom to General Howe, "There is too much Reason to apprehend the

Affair will be soon over."[26]

Dark as the future appeared, there were some bright spots on the horizon. Certainly there was no need for Cramahé to give way to despondency. Developments had occurred during November which should have given him some cause for optimism. Even Cramahé must have realized that the Americans had no means of blockading the harbour of Quebec and that, as long as the river was free of ice, help could always be expected from Great Britain. This very fact had been emphasized by the arrival of H. M. frigate *Lizard* early in November, bearing not only despatches for the governor but also arms, accoutrements and clothing for 6000 men, and £20,000 in specie. With *Lizard* came thirty-seven marines to give added strength to the 130 Irishmen whom Malcolm Fraser, who had been recruiting in Newfoundland for The Royal Highland Emigrants, had picked up in St. John's. Most encouraging of all was the return from Sorel of Allan Maclean and his corps of Emigrants on November 12th. Maclean's men were, nearly all of them, veterans, and Maclean himself was an officer of experience and determination. With these reinforcements the British garrison numbered 1126 men on November 14th, made up of 200 Emigrants and Fusiliers under Maclean, 300 British militia, 480 French Canadian militia, 24 seamen and 90 recruits for the Emigrants and 32 Artificers from Newfoundland.

When he landed at Quebec Colonel Maclean assumed full responsibility for the defence of the city. He put an immediate stop to all talk of negotiation or surrender. But he knew that suppression was not enough. He would have to win the support of the English element. And in so doing he succeeded when Cramahé had failed. He knew far better than the lieutenant governor the kind of arguments that would convince the doubtful and encourage the timid. He pictured Arnold's men as vagabonds and highwaymen come only to plunder and to pillage. He had no lofty philosophy to offer the people of the city about duty and patriotism; he simply appealed to their self-interest, to their desire to save their property. The Americans quickly realized the effect such talk would have — their spies in the city saw to that. They were no tyros in the art of psychological warfare and knew that unless Maclean could be silenced he might well convince the middle class merchants that it was to their interest to support the government cause. "This Villain," wrote one American officer about Maclean, "has worked up the People against us, by representing us as the worst of Banditti . . . This has caused the People to resist."[27] To get them to resist was exactly what Maclean was trying to do; he had already seen enough of the war to know that the Americans, despite their professions that they came as liberators, were as prone as other soldiers, in fact as soldiers of all time, to engage in looting. It did not take much imagination on the part of the Quebec merchants to realize what could happen if Arnold's half-starved, ill-clothed, religiously fanatical army should gain access to the fleshpots of Quebec. Maclean convinced the merchants, or many of them; and the loyal support

A sketch by F. von Germann, showing a British soldier in Canadian winter dress.

afforded Carleton by the British militia when the assault came is to be explained largely by the persuasive propaganda of Allan Maclean.

The starch put into the defence of Quebec by Maclean soon became apparent. Even if Cramahé had once toyed with the idea of surrender — and there is some evidence that he did — he now refused to recognize Arnold's flag of truce, and prevented the American from circulating in Quebec his demand for the surrender of the city. He also rejected Arnold's follow-up letter protesting against the firing of a musket at his envoy. At the Council of War on November 16th Cramahé accepted Maclean's advice to clear away outlying buildings in the suburb of St. Jean and thus deprive the enemy of shelter while at the same time providing the British gunners of the garrison with a suitable field of fire. At the council Maclean revealed a parade state that showed that the garrison totalled no fewer than 1248 men, if one included the marines from *Lizard*, the impressed crews of the improvised vessels of war, and the artificers and the carpenters.[28] It was admitted that there were 5000 people inside the walls, but the reports also showed that there were rations in sufficient quantity which, if distributed, "with the greatest frugality" would last until the middle of May.[29] Quebec might therefore look forward to a siege of six months without undue suffering.

At this point Guy Carleton stepped ashore from *Fell*. At once he assumed the direction of the civil government and the command of the armed forces. Although he had not shown to great advantage as a tactician in Montreal, he was now to demonstrate his skill in civil matters and his obstinacy in military defence, both of which were qualities that came to the fore in the long months to follow. Any misgivings he had about the future never went beyond Dartmouth, and he gave no indication to his subordinates of anything but cool confidence in himself and in Quebec. Maclean might grumble occasionally about the governor's reticence and caution, but that was all. Time was on Carleton's side. All he had to do was to hold out through the winter; relief must inevitably follow the departure of ice from the St. Lawrence and the coming of spring. Thus it was that under Guy Carleton as its directing spirit, and Maclean as its military commander, Quebec settled in for the fourth siege in its history.

The measures taken for the defence of Quebec by Cramahé and Maclean were satisfactory as far as they went, and they met with Carleton's complete approval. All the governor needed to do was to stiffen them up a bit. Cramahé had tried to keep watch on the loose talk of the malcontents and restrict their movements, but he had ventured only to take direct action against Mercier. Carleton, knowing what it had been like in Montreal to have traitors behind his back, wanted none of them in Quebec. He therefore issued a proclamation, within three days of his return, purging the city of its disloyal elements. "Whereas Information has been given me," Carleton's proclamation read, "that some persons resident here have contumaciously refused to enroll their Names in the Militia . . . and that others who had enrolled their names and had for some time carried arms in the Defence and preservation of the City, have lately laid them down; And also that some persons are busy in endeavouring to draw away and alienate the Affections of His Majesty's good and faithfull Subjects . . . for these Reasons, and in order to rid the Town of all useless, disloyal, and treacherous persons," those who would not carry out their military duties were to "quit the Town in four Days" and the limits of the District of Quebec by December 1st "under pain of being treated as Rebels or Spies" if found within these limits.[30] Disgusted and wrathful merchants began to file out of the city. How many, we do not know: but the number was significant enough, including as it did several of those who had been prominent in the political agitation of earlier years, men like John McCord, the publican, who had quarrelled with Carleton over the sale of liquor to the troops; Zachary Macaulay, who had signed the first petition against the Quebec Act; Edward Antill, who immediately rushed off to secure a commission in the invading army as an engineer; John Bondfield, who, ever the merchant, set off for Philadelphia to procure contracts from the Continental Congress; Wells, Murdoch, Stewart, even some of those who had held commissions in the British militia.

The effect of the purge was a salutary one. The cabals ceased and, according to Lieutenant Colonel Henry Caldwell, a former comrade in arms of General Wolfe, who had settled in Quebec and now commanded the British militia in the city, "that order strengthened the garrison considerably. We could guard against open and avowed enemies, but not against those lurking about town." Everybody, even those whose political sympathies had formerly been with the opponents of the government, "seemed zealous for the public service."[31]

Once rid of the unreliable element within the city, Carleton set about regrouping the disparate components of his defence forces. He organized four separate brigades or battle groups. The first comprised all the regulars, the Royal Highland Emigrants, the Fusiliers, and the marines. These he placed under the direct command of Colonel Allan Maclean who continued, at the same time, to act as the governor's second in command. The British militia was placed under Lieutenant Colonel Caldwell; the French Canadian militia under Lieutenant Colonel Noel Voyer; and the seamen, under Captain John Hamilton, master of *Lizard*. With these men Carleton faced the enemy who, on December 4th, retraced their steps from Pointe aux Trembles to Quebec. He planned no offensive action. His strategy was to force the Americans to come to him. Meanwhile he would maintain tight security and admit no flag of truce, no messenger, no communications from the enemy commanders. When they found that neither an Official envoy nor a prostitute could get word into the city, the Americans were reduced to firing arrows with letters attached at the walls in the hope that, somehow, they might reach the people sheltered inside Quebec.

III. Montgomery's and Arnold's Plans for the Assault

It was December 3rd when General Richard Montgomery and his men joined Arnold at Pointe aux Trembles. By virtue of his seniority of rank, Montgomery took command of the combined forces and issued instructions that all the troops should at once resume operations against Quebec. The next day the combined divisions of Montgomery and Arnold made their way down the St. Lawrence to take up their positions before the city. Montgomery chose as his headquarters Holland House, a large, stone house built in the traditional Canadian style, located about two miles south-west of the St. John's gate. Arnold set up his headquarters in the suburb of St. Roch.

Arnold's headquarters in 1775 near Quebec, from a sketch by A. Durie, and published in the *Canadian Illustrated News*, December 26, 1863.

All roads to and from the city were blockaded and companies of troops were spotted at various points across the Plains, extending from Wolfe's Cove to the St. Charles River. The New Yorkers occupied the right of the line, while Morgan's riflemen covered the left at St. Roch. Small detachments were stationed in Beauport and elsewhere to strengthen the cordon around the city. As soon as the envelopment of Quebec was complete, Montgomery sent a flag of truce bearing a letter addressed to Carleton, asking him to surrender and spare himself and the city from the fate which would inevitably befall should he persist in his resistance. The American commander argued that since Quebec was defended only "by a motley crew of sailors, the greatest part our friends, or of citizens who wish to see us within their walls, and a few of the worst troops who ever styled themselves soldiers," surrender was the only reasonable course.[32] It was an inflated letter, a gigantic bluff, for the American army numbered no more than 1000 effectives. Drawing upon Arnold's experience, Montgomery probably did not expect the letter would ever get inside Quebec; for that reason he chose as his emissary an old woman who managed to talk her way through the Palais gate. When the letter was finally delivered to Carleton, he did not read it; he merely burned it unopened. Meanwhile Montgomery wrote another letter, this time intended for the inhabitants of the city, not for the governor, in which he painted a lurid picture of Quebec in flames, of carnage, confusion and plunder, and urged them to take a determined stand against their tyrannical governor. This letter was shot over the walls with an arrow.

Montgomery rightly assumed that he would receive no answer from Carleton and so he set about erecting batteries with the guns he had brought from Montreal. The first of these batteries opened fire on the city on December 9th. Another battery of mortars was placed in St. Roch, behind protecting buildings, only a few hundred yards from the walls. A third, defended by a parapet of ice, was located near the St. John's gate. At the same time American snipers made their way into the ruins of the Intendant's palace in Lower town and, from a small cupola, were able to pick off individual sentinels on the city wall. At first the local people were terrified at what they thought the bombardment could do — some of them probably had in mind the devastation wrought by Wolfe's guns only sixteen years before. They thought that "every shell wou'd inevitably kill a dozen or two of people, & knock down some two or three houses; some were in fears about their tenements, but the greatest part were occupied about the safety of their persons."[33] However, the ineffectiveness of Montgomery's nine and twelve pounders soon convinced the population that it had little to fear, and the disdain it developed for the enemy's cannonade was expressed by Ainslie's entry in his diary for December 11th: "they had anticipated much evil: but after they saw that their bombettes as they called them, did no harm, women and children walked the streets laughing at their former fears."[34] It added to their confidence when they realized that their own guns not only outranged those of their opponents but also carried a heavier weight of metal. Almost immediately it became apparent that the American batteries were just not in a position to compete with those of the fortress, and the efficiency of British counter-battery work was apparent from the casualties and damage suffered by the American guns and gunners. Arnold was driven from his headquarters in St. Roch when his house was riddled with shot, and Montgomery saw his horse killed and his sleigh smashed into "a thousand pieces."[35] As for the American batteries, their shells had no more effect upon the city's walls "than pease wou'd have against a plank," as one citizen put it.[36]

Montgomery was soldier enough to know that he could never hope to take Quebec, particularly at this time of year, by the ordinary methods of siege warfare. The frozen earth made trench-digging impracticable, and the rock underlay discouraged mining in the style approved by Vauban. The American guns were clearly inadequate to the task of breaching the walls of the city or of destroying the morale of the inhabitants. His troops, although they had been provided with new British uniforms from the stocks captured at St. Jean and Chambly, lacked most of the equipment necessary to conduct a campaign in the heart of the Canadian winter. Moreover, there were problems of discipline and morale. Arnold had been having trouble with some of his Connecticut men who were looking forward too eagerly to the early termination of the period of their enlistment, and the ubiquitous

Dr. Isaac Senter, who accompanied Arnold to Quebec and wrote an interesting account of what happened on the journey and at Quebec.

John Brown was running around trying to exploit their discontent to his own advantage. Disease, too, was beginning to take its toll of Yankee strength. Dr. Senter, who had taken over the old General Hospital in St. Roch, noted in his journal on December 23rd, "Not only the small-pox, but the pleurisy, peri-pneumonia, with the other species of pulmonic complaints, were now very prevalent in the army."[37] And they would get worse before they got better. Montgomery's early success in the Richelieu valley had made the conquest of Canada look much too easy, and gave everyone a false sense of certain victory. Far to the south, in Philadelphia, Adams and other members of the Continental Congress wanted Canada and could see no reason why Montgomery should not get it quickly. All that he would have to do would be to bend his "utmost endeavours" to that end. Thus, General Montgomery was left without any choice. Since blockade and siege were not feasible under the circumstances, he would have to take the capital of Canada by storm. In a moment of bravado, more to be associated with Arnold than with Montgomery, the American general declared that he would "dine in Quebec on Christmas day or in Hell."[38]

The troops themselves suspected that there would be an assault. Abner Stocking, a private soldier in Arnold's corps, believed that the bombardment of the city had no other purpose than to "amuse the enemy and conceal our real design . . . an assault." Personally he considered an attempt to storm so formidable a position as that of Quebec "rash and imprudent," but he would not raise his voice against it, lest he "be considered wanting in courage."[39] Caleb Haskell, one of Arnold's fifers, too, was convinced that an assault was in the offing. When Carleton ignored Montgomery's second summons to surrender the fortress, the American commander's bellicose statement that "nothing remains but to pursue vigorous measures for the speedy Reduction of the only Hold possessed by the Ministerial Troops in the Province" merely confirmed a conviction that was generally felt within the besiegers' ranks. The American troops, Montgomery declared, "flushed with continual success, confident of the Justice of their Cause and relying on that Providence which has uniformly protected them, will advance with alacrity to the Attack of Works incapable of being defended by the Wretched Garrison posted behind them, consisting of Sailors unaccustomed to the use of Arms, of Citizens incapable of the Soldier's Duty, and a few miserable Emigrants." Then, in the next sentence he seemed to verify everything that Maclean had said about the Americans and their looting. "The Troops shall have the Effects of the Governor, Garrison, and of such as have been acting in misleading the Inhabitants and distressing the Friends of Liberty, to be equally divided among them. . . ."[40] If this document was truly representative of Montgomery's thinking, he was guilty of a surprising blunder, that of underestimating his opponent.

On December 16th a firm decision to storm Quebec was finally made. At a council of war, a majority of Montgomery's officers expressed their approval of this course of action. Within moments the news of the decision spread through the American camp; some of Arnold's corps were none too enthusiastic about the task — their term of enlistment would soon be over — but when Montgomery explained "the great object" of the enterprise, and that it "would probably lead to peace and the acknowledgement of independence, the fire of patriotism kindled in our breasts," wrote Stocking, and they resolved "to follow wherever he should lead."[41]

During the next few days the cannonade continued, although the American gunners in their "ice" battery on the Plains were getting rather sick of it; they were being pounded to pieces behind a barricade which, although intended to conceal the location of their guns, once discovered, afforded no real protection to the gunners. The weather was, moreover, intensely cold; so cold, said Ainslie, that "no man after having been exposed to the air but ten minutes, cou'd handle his arms to do execution. One's senses were benumb'd. If ever they attack us it will be in mild weather."[42] Nevertheless the preparations for the assault went forward. Bayonets, spears, hatchets, grenades and scaling ladders were made ready. Sprigs of hemlock were also gathered, to be worn in the hats of the American soldiers, in order to distinguish them from their British counterparts, since both were wearing similar uniforms.

Christmas passed without any special observance, Montgomery eating his dinner neither in Quebec nor in the other place. On the 27th the troops were mustered for the assault. The weather had turned warm and the conditions seemed more favourable. But not favourable enough. There was too much light and Montgomery felt compelled to postpone the operation. Fearing that there might be a let-down in the morale of his men as a result of countermanding the order for the assault, he urged them not to be dismayed or disheartened; they would still have a chance to go through with the operation at the first favourable opportunity. Then came the 28th, and the 29th. The weather had turned warmer and it was obvious to all that the attack was near. Finally, it was Saturday, December 30th. It had to be now, for too many troops would be free of military obligations by the beginning of the New Year and there was no assurance they would re-engage. A wind was blowing up the river accompanied by flurries of snow. It was just the kind of weather Montgomery wanted, not too cold, but with sufficient snow to make for poor visibility and render it virtually impossible for the defenders to see the assault troops moving towards the walls. In the late afternoon clouds covered the sky and the blustering snow flurries changed to driving snow. The troops sensed, if they did not know, that their hour was at hand.

The original plan of attack was a simple one. It was discussed at a meeting of company officers at an operations group at Arnold's headquarters on December 23rd. Originally Montgomery had hoped that his cannon might be able to breach the walls of the city and that he would then be able to pour his troops through the gap into the Upper Town where Carleton's administrative and military headquarters were located. Believing that there was still a strong potential fifth column of supporters within the city, such a tactic would, he assumed, bring about a quick and decisive victory. His was the plan of a simple soldier. So, too, was the alternative which he advanced when it became obvious that his artillery was not up to the task of breaching Quebec's walls. The new plan consisted of an assault on the Upper Town at four widely separated points, extending from Cape Diamond to the Palais gate. Three of these assaults would be feints, designed to force Carleton to spread his defenders as thinly as possible. The fourth would be the main attack, and this would be at Cape Diamond, led by Montgomery himself. For it Aaron Burr, his aide-de-camp, would train fifty picked men in the use of scaling ladders. Once these special assault troops had secured a lodgement on the wall, the attack would be pressed home with all possible speed and energy. At this point, however, Edward Antill and James Price suggested still another line of attack. They believed the main objective should be the Lower Town. Here were to be found the warehouses and the stocks of merchandise belonging to the civilian merchants of Quebec, who, once they saw their property in danger, would combine to bring pressure to bear upon Carleton to force him into agreeing to a surrender.[43] This plan had the merit of being based upon the conviction, shared by every American from Adams to Washington, that the bulk of the population in Canada, English as well as French, was secretly in sympathy with the aims and object of the American rebellion. It had, however, a distinct weakness from the military point of view. The occupation of the Lower Town, even if it did give the Americans control of the merchants' warehouses, did not bring them into the Upper Town where Carleton's army would remain intact. It still left the Americans

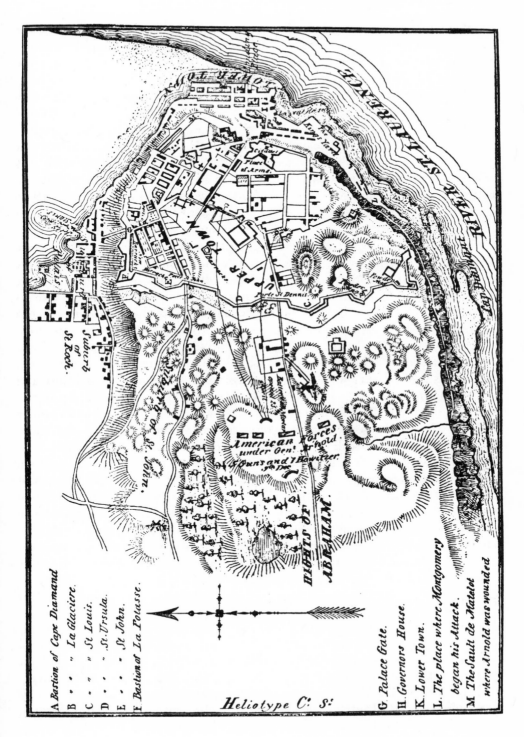

A sketch map of Quebec, 1775.

the difficult task of trying to continue the assault up the hill from the Lower Town against an enemy possessing all the advantages of position. Somehow, Montgomery would have to force Carleton into battle if the Americans were to obtain the decisive victory they desired.

Between the time the initial plan of attack was discussed and the day the attack was launched, two minor events occurred which necessitated a change in Montgomery's intended way of proceeding. The escape of a British prisoner from the enemy's camp and the arrival in Quebec of an American deserter revealed to Carleton not only that an assault was in the offing, but where the main thrust of the attack was to be. Aware of the fact that the British knew his plan, Montgomery made several modifications at the last moment. The assault, as projected for the night of December 30-31st, was to be centered upon the Lower Town. Montgomery would lead his New York troops along the narrow road below Cape Diamond, moving into the Lower Town from the southwest, while Arnold, with the main body of Americans, would push through St. Roch, past the Sault au Matelot, entering Lower Town from the opposite direction. The two forces would then join hands to force their way into the Upper Town, should that be necessary, in the confusion attending the burning of the Lower Town and with the assistance of collaborators inside the city who would come to the support of the American troops. These manoeuvres would have the effect both of terrifying the English merchants into quick submission and forcing Carleton into the battle Montgomery wanted, and had to have. As a cover, or deception scheme, Livingston's Canadians, with a few American provincials under Brown, would carry out a noisy demonstration outside the St. John's gate. For success this plan really rested upon surprise, not strategical but tactical. At least it was a tactical surprise that Montgomery hoped to achieve, if we may judge from a letter he wrote just prior to the fatal attack; "Masters of our secret, we may select a particular time and place for attack; and to repel this the garrison must be prepared at all times and places — a circumstance which will impose upon it incessant watching and labour by day and by night, which, in its undisciplined state, must breed discontent, that may compel Carleton to capitulate, or perhaps to make an attempt to drive us off. In this last idea there is a glimmering of hope."[44]

IV. The American Defeat before Quebec

As far as the defenders of Quebec were concerned, it was not a question of whether an assault would be made, but when and where. And this vital information was placed in Carleton's hands before the attack actually took place. On December 23rd a certain Wolf, a clerk in the service of Lieutenant Colonel Caldwell, who had been taken prisoner by the Americans, by pretending to be drunk, escaped and brought word to the city that the Americans were accumulating scaling ladders and would probably attack that very night.[45] This was confirmed by an American deserter who slipped into

An American rifleman at the time of the Revolution. He carries the "Death or Liberty" badge on his headdress.

Quebec the same day. Meanwhile the defenders had not been idle. They had repaired the merlons and the embrasures on the walls, laid gun platforms, repaired the picketing at Cape Diamond and the Hotel Dieu, erected barriers at the extremities of the Lower Town at Sault au Matelot and Près de Ville and strengthened them with cannon. Now they set about erecting barriers between the Upper and the Lower Town, mounted a series of lights on the walls to illuminate the ditch and the glacis, particularly in the vicinity of the Cape Diamond bastion, and placed additional ordnance in each of the bastions facing westward towards the Plains. Then, on the 24th came another deserter who indicated that the main American thrust would come through the Lower Town. From this moment on the Quebec garrison was constantly on the alert and Carleton and Maclean slept at the Recollet convent fully clothed. The officers and soldiers likewise lay in their clothes in the barracks. Everyone was watching the weather, knowing that it would, in fact, determine the timing of the assault. On the 29th, still another deserter came in with information. This man was, said Ainslie "an intelligent fellow, an Irishman"[46] who confirmed everything that Carleton already knew and stated categorically that Montgomery would move "on the first dark night." He did, in the early hours of December 31st.

About 4 A.M. Captain Malcolm Fraser of The Royal Highland Emigrants was making his rounds in the Upper Town.[47] The morning was very dark and the driving snow not only tended to reduce visibility but also to muffle sound. Suddenly he saw flashes of light in the sky. On making enquiries from the sentries he learned that they too had seen lights for some time in the direction of the Plains, but had heard no sounds nor detected any movement. They did not know what the lights meant. Neither did Fraser, but he had his suspicions. He therefore ordered the guards and pickets to stand to their arms and rushed to give the alarm. Drums beat and bells rang and within a short time the whole garrison was under arms. At this point two rockets shot into the sky from the foot of Cape Diamond. The American cannon began throwing shells into the city and musket fire was heard in the vicinity of the Cape Diamond bastion and the St. John's gate.

Below the Upper Town, between the cliff and the river, ran a small road (rue Petit Champlain) which was connected with the Upper Town by what is today the stairway leading to the Côte de la Montagne. It was wide enough to handle vehicular traffic and continued past the King's Wharf to a point near Cape Diamond, then known as Près de Ville. Here the road narrowed and became no more than a trail skirting the rocks on one side and bounded by the river on the other. Even in summer it was rough and difficult and could accommodate no more than three or four men abreast. At this time the river was much closer to the cliff than it now is, for much of the present Lower Town rests on land filled in during the nineteenth and twentieth centuries for commercial purposes. This meant that in 1775 neither Montgomery nor Arnold had much room to manoeuvre, unless he was prepared to move over the ice, as some of Arnold's men actually did. For this reason it was impossible for them to outflank the defence posts at Près de Ville and Sault au Matelot. It was along this trail that General Montgomery began his approach to Quebec on the morning of December 31st with a small force of men drawn from the 1st, 2nd and 3rd Regiments of New York. He could make his way only very slowly and with difficulty, owing to the deep snow and the huge cakes of ice which had been thrown up by the movement of the tide in the river. By the time he reached the first obstacle at Près de Ville, a strong picket fence, he was behind schedule. But it did not seem to matter very much. Montgomery could detect no sign of any defenders at the barricade and set his carpenters to sawing an opening through the obstacle. This they were able to do without arousing attention, and screened from view by the precipice above, the American attackers moved forward a short distance to a second picket barricade. Watching nervously, Montgomery again ordered his carpenters to remove a few pickets. It all seemed very easy, but every moment's delay increased the chances of discovery. In his impatience Montgomery seized one of the pickets himself to push it out of the way, and then, with his aides and staff officers, stepped through the opening. Some distance behind him, the Yankees were just beginning to struggle through the narrow opening in the first barricade. Suddenly one of Montgomery's officers detected the outlines of a house nearby belonging to one Simon Fraser. The question that must

Death of General Montgomery in the attack on Quebec, oil on canvas, by the American painter, John Trumbull (1756-1843). A highly imaginative and romanticized version of the American commander's death.

A British version of the death of Montgomery, designed by E. F. Burney and engraved by G. Terry, 1789. It makes a greater effort to adhere to historical fact than the Trumbull painting, but can scarcely be considered as an accurate portrayal of what happened.

have rushed to Montgomery's mind was whether it was occupied. Obviously, however, there was no time to waste in speculation, and with a shout, "Push on, brave boys; Quebec is ours," the American general dashed forward. Instantly there was a loud explosion. Canister and grape streamed through the air from Fraser's house, followed by further shots and discharge of musketry. Montgomery, Macpherson, Cheeseman, their Canadian guide, and eight others were hurled to the ground, torn and bleeding. Aaron Burr was left standing, dazed but unhurt. Colonel Donald Campbell, upon whom the command now devolved, was utterly incapable of coping with the situation in which he found himself, and took the easiest way out. He grabbed Burr and ran. When he encountered his troops he ordered them to withdraw. An army derives its courage from that of its leaders, and with Montgomery dead and Campbell in a panic, the New Yorkers became a mob rather than an army. They too turned and ran, leaving behind them their dead and wounded in the blood-spattered snow. Scrambling along the narrow roadway, slipping and falling on the ice and snow, they wanted nothing more than to put as much distance as possible between themselves and the opponents they had hoped to overcome by surprise. But they, not the defenders, had been taken by surprise, and it was only a matter of minutes before the only sounds to be heard were the groans of the wounded and the howling of the wind.

The house at Près de Ville was the first defended post Montgomery encountered. He had been hidden from the sight of the garrison in the blockhouse high up on Cape Diamond, and the defenders who had taken post in Simon Fraser's house, "The Pot Ash," had had no warning of the American approach. They were not a large or very well disciplined group. There were only about thirty of them, French Canadian militia under the command of two militia officers, Captain Chabot and Lieutenant Alexandre Picard, and a handful of seamen commanded by a civilian ship's master, Captain Barnsfare, whose services had been commandeered by Cramahé, and John Coffin, a volunteer. Such a post was not likely to have offered serious resistance to an attack strongly pressed home. But the defenders were on the alert and had all the advantage of surprise, and they did what they were expected to do. Even so, they were sufficiently jittery that later in the morning when they received word that Arnold had broken through behind them, they were disposed to pull out and run for the Upper Town. Fortunately, however, some sense of discipline was restored and they turned a couple of their guns around and awaited a second attack. Some of the garrison went out to examine the bodies in the snow and found Montgomery's orderly sergeant, desperately wounded, but still living. On being asked whether his commanding officer had been killed, the sergeant returned an evasive answer. Even though he had but a short time to live, he would give no satisfaction to those whom he regarded as his enemies. It was not until some hours afterwards, when Carleton sent an American prisoner to look at the bodies at Près de Ville, that he learned that among those who had died in the opening minutes of the assault had been the commanding general of the American army.

Meanwhile Benedict Arnold, with the main body numbering about 700, had started to bring his men in from the outlying posts and assemble them in the suburb of St. Roch about two hours after midnight. There were delays as the various companies came in to report and when, about 4 A.M., Dearborn had not yet arrived, Arnold decided to wait no longer and gave orders for his corps to move to the attack. Arnold himself led off with a hundred men, breaking trail in the snow. Behind him came the gunners with a brass cannon on a sled; then Morgan, and then the various battalion companies which had followed him from Fort Western to Quebec. The going was difficult, for the snow inside the town was heavier than it was on the Plains, and the pathway was almost imperceptible as the footprints of the leading "forlorn hope" soon filled with drifting snow. Moving along, Indian file, the men were grateful for the shelter afforded by the cliff, and even for the snow which obscured their movements; but the snow was a doubtful blessing, for it had a tendency to get into the locks of their weapons and to render them useless when they were most needed. As Arnold's column reached the ascent to the Palais gate, its presence was detected by the guards on the wall, and the American troops found themselves exposed to musket fire and grenades to which, John Henry moaned, they were unable to reply. The guards on the walls were "sightless to us," wrote Henry, "We could see nothing but the blaze from the muzzles of their muskets." What was even more significant was the fact that this musket fire indicated that the Quebec garrison was now awake and ready to receive the expected assault. There was, however,

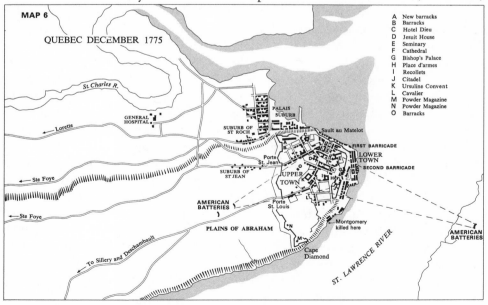

MAP 6

QUEBEC DECEMBER 1775

A New barracks
B Barracks
C Hotel Dieu
D Jesuit House
E Seminary
F Cathedral
G Bishop's Palace
H Place d'armes
I Recollets
J Citadel
K Ursuline Convent
L Cavalier
M Powder Magazine
N Powder Magazine
O Barracks

Daniel Morgan, who commanded the American riflemen under Benedict Arnold and whose hesitation at the Sault au Matelot led to his surrender, December 31, 1775.

no question of Arnold's pulling back at this point. Montgomery, he believed, was moving in his direction, and the success of the whole operation depended upon a co-ordinated effort. Arnold's men therefore ran the gauntlet of the fire upon the walls, past the Hôtel Dieu, the Canotière, Sous le Cap, and around the sharp projection which, in those days, stuck out into the waters of the river, and which was called the Sault au Matelot. Here, at last, they found the snowbound warehouses, buildings and dockyards about which the English merchants in the city were believed to be particularly sensitive.

It was here the attackers encountered their first obstacle. It was a barricade across the east end of Sault au Matelot street, a short narrow road, lined with buildings on either side, just below the ramparts on which stood the old Séminaire de Québec. Across the entrance to this street the defenders had placed a barrier and mounted two small cannon. When Arnold saw it he ordered the storming party to charge forward on the double and to seize the portholes in the barricade and fire through them at the defenders behind it. According to Henry, this initial brush with the British lasted only a few minutes, but was short and sharp while it lasted. Arnold was hit by a bullet just below the knee, and fell to the ground. But his men had caught something of his energy, and the British guard quickly laid down their arms which were as quickly seized by their captors because their own had powder pans filled with snow. The captain of the guard, apparently, simulated drunkenness to excuse his supine conduct, although there were some who were inclined to believe that he had been secretly in sympathy with the Americans from the outset.[48] Once through the barricade, the Americans, now under the command of the rifleman, Daniel Morgan, surged into the Sault au Matelot where they caught several students from the seminary on their way to reinforce the second barricade, which was located at the far end of the street blocking the exit from Sault au Matelot.

For the moment Morgan hesitated. He had outstripped most of the main body and he had to provide escorts for the prisoners he had taken. Moreover his cannon had not arrived. It had been abandoned before the American troops had rounded the Sault au Matelot. What Morgan did not know was that some of the companies belonging to the main body had lost their way wandering about through the buildings and warehouses, and had no clear idea of where they were supposed to be. Moreover, the casualties from the gunfire from the walls had been greater than anticipated and Dearborn, coming up late, noted in his journal, "we met the wounded men very thick."[49] Nor did he realize the impact that the sight of a wounded Arnold, hobbling back to Senter's hospital, held up by two officers, might have upon the men of the rear companies. Despite Arnold's words of encouragement to the troops whom he passed, the very sight of the man who had led them over the Kennebec, dragging his useless leg after him "dampen'd their spirits." John Henry, who did not like Arnold, admitted as much, and recorded that too many soldiers muttered audibly, "We are sold."[50] In his moment of hesitation, Morgan lost the initiative, and in losing that he lost Quebec. In these few minutes the tide of battle turned against the Americans.

In the Upper Town the situation was well in hand. As soon as the troops had assembled in consequence of Fraser's warning, Maclean had ordered Colonel Caldwell and a number of British militia to go to Cape Diamond to lend whatever support might be required there. Caldwell found that the defenders at Cape Diamond had no need of reinforcements and on his own initiative led his men to the St. Louis gate and then to the St. John's gate. En route he encountered a picket of Fusiliers and Emigrants whom he ordered to headquarters to receive orders for their disposition. Caldwell considered that no real threat was developing from the Plains and that the militia guards and gunners on the walls were thoroughly capable of handling the noisy demonstration of Livingston and Brown, and then proceeded to the Palais gate. Strengthening his militia with a few Emigrants under Captain John Nairne, Caldwell then made his way into the Lower Town by the rue de la Montagne which led directly to the second barrier at the south end of Sault au Matelot Street. Meanwhile Carleton had been informed by Maclean of the serious situation developing in the Sault au Matelot. He had, therefore, ordered some 200 men to take position at the second barrier. These included a few Fusiliers of the 7th Regiment and a number of French Canadian militia under Colonel Voyer and Captain Alexandre Dumas. When they reached the barricade they found the Americans were already in the street, but fortunately they had halted and not yet rushed to the assault. Somewhat unsteady at the outset, the defenders welcomed the appearance of Caldwell's reinforcements. Moreover, Caldwell's military experience was a great advantage at this critical juncture. Taking over command, Caldwell placed his men in strategic defence locations at the barricade and sighted a cannon to fire over the top. The Fusiliers he ranged in line with bayonets drawn to meet the threat that would develop should the Americans attempt to scale the barricade.

The assailants had, in fact, brought scaling ladders with them for this very purpose. They had had no need to use them at the first barricade, but with the arrival of Greene's men with Bigelow and Meigs, Morgan plunged forward to the attack. Desperate efforts were made to get the ladders up against the second barricade, but faced with a withering fire from the defenders, the Americans were unable to clamber over it. A defender, however, a huge giant of a Canadian, Charles Charland by name, seized one of the American ladders, wrested it from the enemy, and placed it up against the gable end of a house facing the Sault au Matelot. Immediately Nairne and François Dambourgès, with a party of Emigrants and Canadians, climbed the ladder and entered the house in time to expel, at the point of a bayonet, a group of Americans who had forced their way in the front door. Other defenders also mounted the ladder and took up positions at the windows of the upstairs rooms to fire at the milling crowd below. In order to find cover from the British fire, a number of the Americans sought refuge in some houses bordering the Sault au Matelot, and the fighting continued in the upper stories as well as in the street. One by one Morgan's officers fell back, killed or wounded, but Morgan, "brave to temerity" as Henry wrote of him, stormed and raged and drove his men until all hope of success had vanished from their hearts.

Meanwhile Carleton, seizing the initiative at the critical moment, had ordered Captain George Lawes to take a force and sally forth into the Lower Town from the Palais gate. Accompanied by Captain McDougall and a detachment of Emigrants, and Captain Hamilton with some seamen from *Lizard*, he descended the hill by the Palais road, only to run into the bewildered company commanded by Dearborn, who, lost in the snow and among the buildings of St. Roch, was still trying to make contact with Morgan. After a sharp exchange of fire, Dearborn gave up and Lawes, after sending a detachment to eliminate the American battery in St. Roch which had annoyed the garrison in the Upper Town for some days, proceeded around the Sault au Matelot, to catch the beleaguered Morgan in the rear. Morgan realized his predicament, but still hoping for help from Montgomery, of whose death he was ignorant, continued to offer a firm resistance. Lawes, "impatient to be among them . . . got before his men" and was seized by several Americans, who disarmed him. But when they saw British gunners unlimbering their field gun and preparing to fire up the narrow street, they decided to give themselves up to McDougall and Nairne. They were trapped and they knew it. Others took to their heels and fled over treacherous ice with its snow-covered cracks and air holes, while a few crawled into cupboards and attics in the hope that they might, in this way, evade

A half-tone plate engraved by F. H. Wellington from a drawing by Sydney Adamson entitled "Withstanding the Attack of Arnold's Men at the Second Barrier." It shows the Fusiliers prepared to meet the assaulting American troops as they attempted to climb the barrier, with the Canadian militia firing at the enemy from the upper windows.

detection. Morgan, bitter in his defeat, and insulting to his victors to the end, surrendered his sword to a black-robed priest, rather than yield it to a red-coated British soldier. Lawes's other detachment penetrated to St. Roch and captured eight coehorn mortars and one field six pounder on a sleigh. Then, "to the great joy of the whole town" they set fire to those buildings, including the Intendant's palace, which had been used to shelter American gunners and snipers. The battle was over and the day had been won. "A glorious day for us, as compleat a little victory as ever was gained,"[51] was how one of Carleton's artillery officers described it.

It was, indeed, a "compleat" victory. The flower of the American army before Quebec, the men of Arnold's corps, had given up and were slowly making their way to the improvised prisons in Quebec. Even in defeat they impressed Finlay, one of the British residents of Quebec, who described them as "really fine looking fellows. They had, most of them, papers in front of their caps, on which were the words 'Liberty or Death'";[52] 389 of them had lost their liberty; another 42 were wounded and 30 had found death, for a total of 461 casualties. The number of the killed was probably larger than these official figures indicated. Maclean wrote in May that another twenty bodies had been found after the snows had melted in the spring; and there were accounts of others who had lost their lives by falling through the ice during their mad flight from the Sault au Matelot. Henry stated in his journal, "of commissioned officers we had six killed, five wounded: and of non-commissioned officers and privates at least one hundred and fifty killed and fifty or sixty wounded."[53] Perhaps a more accurate statement is that given in a letter from Brigadier General Wooster to Seth Warner, dated January 12th, 1776: "With the greatest distress of Mind, I now sit down to acquaint you of the Event, of an unfortunate attack made upon Quebec, between the Hours of 4 and 6 of the Morning of the 31st of December. Unfortunate indeed, for in it fell our brave General Montgomery, his Aid de Camp McPherson, Captain Cheeseman, Capt. Hendricks of the Riflemen, and 2 or 3 Subaltern Officers, and between 60 and 100 Privates, the number not certainly known, and about 300 Officers and Soldiers taken Prisoners, amongst which are Lieut. Col. Green, Major Bigalow, Major Meigs and a number of Captains and inferior Officers, Col. Arnold was wounded in the leg in the Beginning of the Action, as was Major Ogden in the shoulder, and brought off to the General Hospital."[54] The British casualties were comparatively light. Carleton reported to General Howe that he had lost only one lieutenant of the Navy "doing Duty as a Captain in the Garrison," and four or five rank and file wounded of whom two subsequently died.[55] Finlay mentioned specifically the loss of Captain Anderson, the naval officer to whom Carleton made reference, five men killed and one wounded. One of the killed was a soldier of the French Canadian militia and the rest were seamen and British militia; among the latter was a master ship-builder by the name of Fraser. Anderson and Fraser, along with Brigadier General Montgomery, who, unlike those who had fallen with him at Près de Ville, had "a genteel coffin," were buried quietly in Quebec on January 4th, 1776.

V. The Relief of Quebec, May 6th, 1776

After repelling his assailants so conclusively it would have been natural for Carleton to have launched a counter-attack against the Americans while they were still off balance, and while Arnold was incapable of leading them in battle. But, decisive as he had been in a defensive action, Carleton was never the man to act with decision in the offense. He therefore chose to remain within the walls of Quebec and to allow the Americans to regroup and to make good the losses they had suffered. As long as he stayed inside Quebec he felt secure. Despite the fact that his militia, both French Canadian and British, had fought well and his regulars had suffered virtually no casualties, he was not of a mind to risk them in an engagement. Nevertheless, he took every precaution to maintain vigilance in defence. He had the civilian population well in hand, since he controlled the issue of rations from the government stores; and he had no shortages to fear except fuel, and that could be obtained by small military parties foraging in the neighbouring suburbs. He was well provided with ordnance. No fewer than 148 cannon were in place on May 1st, poking their iron noses through the embrasures in the walls, as compared with the six that were in position when the siege began in November. At the same time he kept the outer wall well lighted, with fireballs burning from dusk to dawn, and lanterns suspended on

François Dambourgès who served with distinction against the Americans during the assault on Quebec, and who subsequently was commissioned in The Royal Highland Emigrants.

poles extending over the ditch. Anticipating a possible attack against his ships, should the river freeze in its entirety, he returned the cannon he had taken from them earlier and cut a trench in the ice at Près de Ville to prevent attacking parties from outflanking the defences. He also destroyed the houses lining Sault au Matelot street.

Meanwhile Carleton kept the American prisoners under lock and key inside the Upper Town. The officers were placed in the seminary and the other ranks in the monastery and college of the Recollets. Subsequently the latter were transferred to the Dauphin jail, a building which had been constructed on the model of the Bastille and which stood some three hundred yards from the St. John's gate. On the whole the prisoners appear to have been well treated. Carleton was a humane man. Whatever vengeance he may have sought against his political opponents, he was never the kind of man to relish the role of jailor. The officers were allowed to recover their baggage and those prisoners of British birth were given a chance to enlist in Maclean's Royal Highland Emigrants as an alternative to being sent to England to stand trial for treason. About ninety-four, most of them Irishmen, chose to accept the offer and did regular tours of guard duty with the other members of the regiment. Some, of course, were unable to resist the opportunity this afforded them of making a dash for freedom, and went over the wall. Indeed, so frequent did these desertions become that Carleton, in March, "disarmed and disuniformed" the new recruits and sent them to the holds of the ships in the harbour. Meanwhile, plans were made by the American prisoners-of-war to break out of the Dauphin jail. Their idea was to make a sudden dash and, in the confusion, to obtain arms and overpower the guard at the nearby St. John's gate. However, when a jailor discovered that a lock and several hinges had been tampered with, he reported it to the authorities, and then one of the prisoners, seeking to curry favour, revealed the details of the plot. The outcome was that the prisoners were placed in foot-irons and handcuffs. Among the officers, a scheme to escape from the seminary ended in the despatch of Simeon Thayer, Oliver Hanchet and Samuel Lockwood to the hold of Henry Laforce's armed sloop. Their incarceration was of short duration. It lasted only from April 26th to May 6th when they were once more returned to the seminary.

Outside Quebec all was gloom and discouragement. Arnold was weak from loss of blood, but when rumours reached him that a sortie was to be expected from the fortress, he buckled on his sword and ordered muskets to be placed within the reach of every wounded man. It was the gesture of desperation, and yet typical of Arnold's panache. In a more sober mood he sent a message to Brigadier General Wooster by Antill, outlining the events at Quebec and announcing his resignation of his command to Colonel Donald Campbell. Reporting the condition of his troops, he told Wooster that his overall strength was 800 men, including 200 Canadians under Livingston; but he admitted that nearly all his soldiers were dispirited and that many of them were anxious to return home. "For God's sake," he wrote, "order as many men down as you can possibly spare, consistent with the safety of Montreal, and all the mortars, howitzers, and shells, that you can possibly bring." Then he added bitterly, "I hope you will stop every rascal who has deserted us, and bring him back again."[56]

Arnold's retirement in favour of Campbell did not, however, meet with the approval of the army. Arnold's officers got together, discussed the matter, and asked Arnold to withdraw his resignation. They had no respect for Campbell and attributed to his cowardice the failure of Montgomery's thrust at Près de Ville. They affirmed their conviction that only Arnold was capable of restoring order to the army and fighting zeal to the men. Without him as their leader, who could possibly sustain their interest in a dreary and apparently futile siege? Arnold agreed. He resumed his command on January 24th and received an injection of hope when the first of a series of reinforcement drafts from Montreal and from the colonies reached the American camp. If these could be maintained, he might be able to resume the siege in a more efficient fashion, for Arnold knew that despite his figure of 800, Wooster was nearer the truth when he reported to Washington that Arnold had no more than 350 American soldiers who could be called effective, not counting the Canadians whose zeal for the American cause seemed to be diminishing with the use of paper money for payment rather than hard cash. However, Congress still had faith in Canadian support, and on January 24th Moses Hazen was given a commission as colonel to raise a second regiment of Canadian volunteers. Hazen attempted to drum up men in Montreal, but recruits came in slowly and by the end of February he had obtained only 150 men. Meanwhile Antill, who acted as Hazen's lieutenant colonel, and Duggan were actively engaged in running around among the various parishes of La Beauce, competing in their efforts to persuade Canadian militiamen to throw in their lot with the continental idea and the Continental Army. When Duggan left the Quebec region in March, his place as a recruiting agent was taken by Clément Gosselin and Pierre Ayotte. Between them Livingston and Hazen probably mustered about 500 men.[57]

For four months, Arnold maintained an ineffective siege which in no way injured Carleton, and an equally ineffective battle against the inroads of smallpox. Why did he not withdraw to Montreal, where conditions would have been better both for himself and his men and where he would have been nearer the main source of his reinforcements? The explanation lies partly in the unyielding temperament of the man himself, and partly in the fact that his orders from Washington to remain where he was were imperative. This seems to be the gist of Washington's letter to Arnold of January 27th which stated, "I need not mention to you the great importance of this place (Quebec), and the consequent possession of all Canada, in the scale of American affairs. . . . The glorious work must be accomplished in the course of this winter, otherwise it will become difficult, most probably impracticable; for the administration, knowing it will be impossible ever to reduce us to a state of slavery and arbitrary rule without it, will certainly send a large reinforcement thither in the spring. I am fully convinced that your exertions will be invariably directed to this grand object. . . ."[58]

Arnold, however, never did undertake another assault against Quebec. Until October he did not fight another battle against Carleton or Carleton's men, unless we include the engagement between his troops and the vanguard of a loyalist contingent of French Canadians from the parishes below Quebec raised by the Sieur de Beaujeu, a former officer of Montcalm's, living in retirement on the Isle aux Grues. This event took place at Saint Pierre du Sud, near Beaumont on March 25th. Meanwhile, Arnold simply maintained the semblance of a siege, while asking to be replaced by a senior officer of general rank, and begging for further reinforcements. Finally, on March 31st, after suffering another injury to his leg by a fall from his horse, he was relieved of his command by Brigadier General Wooster.

The siege, in fact, was nearly over. With the approach of spring every man around Quebec was keeping his eyes turned eastwards down the St. Lawrence. Those in Quebec itself thought they saw British ships approaching on the evening of May 3rd when they descried a vessel in full sail moving up the river in the moonlight. But it turned out to be an enemy fire-ship which, being "well garnish'd in all parts with shells, grenades, petards, pots a feu" failed to reach the harbour and merely provided the onlookers with an interesting display of pyrotechnics. Three days later, on May 6th, the first ship of the relief fleet from Great Britain did arrive. She was the frigate *Surprise*; and in her wake came *Isis* and the sloop-of-war, *Martin*. Ainslie described the scene: "the news soon reached every pillow in town, people half-dress'd ran down to the Grand battery to feast their eyes. . . ." Troops were immediately landed, and without any delay were joined by troops, militia and regulars, from the garrison of Quebec. With Carleton in command and Maclean's Emigrants in the van, the whole force marched out of the city to the Plains. The Americans offered no resistance; they were on the run, leaving their guns, mortars, field pieces, muskets, even their orderly books and clothing behind them. Wrote Ainslie, "As we pursued them we found the road strew'd with arms, cartridges, cloaths, bread, pork."[59] Carleton did not move fast enough to force a battle; he was content to frighten the enemy and to let some of Maclean's Highlanders have the fun of eating the dinner that the American officers had prepared for themselves but had had no opportunity to enjoy.[60]

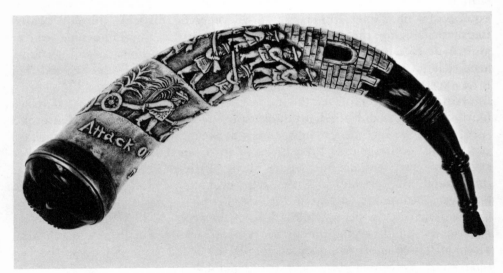

A powder horn at the Canadian War Museum, beautifully and deeply carved, according to legend, by a soldier in Montgomery's army who later became a Trappist monk. In an ascending spiral are carved vignettes of the attack on Quebec, December 31, 1775. There is a collar with the words "monk of La Trappe," and a wooden face carved in the end.

IV Canada Liberated 1776

I. Congress Sends Three Commissioners to Canada

One of the assumptions which underlay the American offensive of 1775 was that the bulk of the French-speaking population of Canada would welcome the American invaders as liberators, and that they would not only flock to support American arms, but would also seek political affiliation with the Continental Congress. During the early days of the invasion this assumption appeared to be founded upon fact. Although the French Canadians in the Richelieu Valley had not turned out in great numbers to join Livingston's (and later Hazen's) regiment, a number of them had, nevertheless, taken an active part in Allen's fiasco at Montreal, supported Brown and Livingston in front of Chambly, provided the Americans with food and transport (at a price), and refused to respond to Carleton's appeals for help. In Beauce they had greeted Arnold warmly. One of the Quebec collaborators, John Bondfield, was saying no more than the truth when he asserted that Arnold's men would never have reached Quebec "had not the Canadians opened the Road and led them by the hand to the very gates of the Capital."[1] And all of this despite the fulminations of Bishop Briand and his *mandements* condemning the American rebellion and urging the habitants to take up arms for the king. Even after the débâcle of Quebec, men like Captain Merlet of Ile Dupas, Maurice Desdevens at Pointe aux Trembles, Philippe Baronnet at Deschambault, Etienne Parent in Beauce, Clément Gosselin and Germain Dionne at Sainte Anne de la Pocatière, took an active part in recruiting men for the American-sponsored battalions, and in intimidating those of their parishes who were inclined to support the government. Even more belligerent than the men were two women, the widow Gaboury and the wife of Augustin Chabot, both of whom were known by the soubriquet of "la reine de Hongrie."[2]

But French Canadian support for the invasion was more apparent than real and more imaginary than apparent. Most of the French Canadians remained neutral and non-committal. One of the most active collaborators, Christophe Pélissier, the proprietor of the Forges at Trois Rivières, admitted as much when he stated that only a handful of French Canadians gave active backing to the American forces during 1775-1776. And even that encouragement began to wane after Montgomery's failure and a taste of American military administration in Montreal.

Montgomery, during his short stay in Montreal, had made a favourable impression. However, his objective was Quebec and when he left for Quebec, David Wooster had taken over responsibility for both the military and political government of Montreal and its environs. Wooster, however, was a dull man. Bluff and hearty to his soldiers, he was zealous and wholly unimaginative in his management of the civilian population of Canada. His first act was harmless enough. It was to distribute George Washington's letter promising, in terms of brotherly affection, that none of the inhabitants of Canada should suffer in person or in property as a result of the American military occupation. The Americans were, he declared, inspired by the idea of liberty and had a mission from "that Being in whose hands are all human events" to destroy the "ravages" of tyranny.[3] However, with the return of Thomas Walker to Montreal, American political policy soon departed from the lofty principles which had appeared in Washington's letter. Wooster became, in fact, the tool of the revengeful Walker, and Wooster's first act after he learned of Montgomery's defeat and death was to order the arrest of twelve prominent Montreal citizens, nearly all of them French Canadians, who were known to be supporters of the Crown, such as Pierre Panet, Simon Sanguinet, William Gray, Joseph Sanguinet, Laurent Ermatinger and St. George Dupré. This arbitrary action brought forth a strong protest from their fellow citizens. Where was the liberty of which the Americans boasted? Was it all just a masquerade? Was not Wooster's action a direct violation of the terms of the surrender granted by Montgomery? Wooster yielded but he reminded Montrealers that he had a list of sixty-four suspects who might at any time be sent to prisons in the colonies.[4]

It was not in Wooster's nature to woo and conciliate when blunt action would, he believed, be more effective. Hence, on January 6th, 1776, he issued a public warning that any person seeking to injure the cause of Congress by word or deed, or send help of any kind to the garrison at Quebec, or who disobeyed the American authorities, would be considered a traitor and would be punished accordingly. A notice to this effect was posted on all churches in the occupied territory south and east of Montreal. Ten days later, Wooster ordered the disarming of three Montreal suburbs regarded as sympathetic to the government. To ensure the good behaviour of the people he ordered the surrender of Hertel de Rouville and William Gray as hostages. When this action produced another protest, Wooster told the people of the town that he looked upon all of them as enemies and rascals. This was not an assurance of good will likely to win a sympathetic response;

General Wooster, whose administration of Montreal during the American occupation 1775-1776 helped turn even sympathetic opinion against the Americans.

neither was his order to the captains of militia to surrender their British commissions. But Wooster was determined to root out all support for Carleton and the Crown. The old militia was to be done away with and new companies were to be formed in which the men would elect their officers. These officers would then receive commissions from Congress. When Dufy-Desaunier, Neveu-Sevestre, St. George Dupré, of the French militia and William Gray of the British militia refused to give up their commissions on the grounds that they were personal property of a kind the Americans had promised to respect, they were arrested and were sent to be imprisoned in Fort Chambly.

Actions like these only served to alienate a population already growing resentful of the presence of an unruly alien army in their midst, commanded by an unsympathetic general. Pélissier had warned Wooster to be careful to respect the clergy and the Roman Catholic faith. Even if some of the French Canadians had resisted the political admonitions of Bishop Briand, they were still Catholics and would tolerate no interference with their church. Wooster paid little heed to this sound advice, and his order to close "the Mass houses" on Christmas Eve was an act of incredible stupidity. Montgomery had been aware of the fact that the clergy were working against him and that heavy ecclesiastical pressures were being brought on Canadians to remain out of the rebellion, but he had had the good judgement to avoid a head-on collision with the Roman Catholic church. However, Wooster was too good a Protestant to show any sympathy to a religious body which his own Puritan army chaplains were calling the Antichrist, and whose clergy refused the sacraments to those who supported the American rebellion. "The clergy (are) our bitter Enemies," was Arnold's view, and Moses Hazen felt much the same way when he reported to Arnold that they were "unanimous . . . against our cause."[5]

And then there was the question of payment for supplies purchased from the civilian population. Washington's orders to Arnold concerning this matter had been emphatic: "You will be particularly careful to pay the full value for all provisions, or other accommodations, which the Canadians may provide for you on your march."[6] However, the failure of Congress to provide army commanders with the specie necessary to do this, presented both Arnold and Montgomery with almost unsurmountable difficulties. The only alternative was paper notes, and the Canadians had had enough of paper money during the Seven Years' War; they were not prepared to accept it again. Inflation and its attendant evils held no charms for them. But what else had the Americans to offer, once they had exhausted the monies they had brought from the colonies and the loans they had obtained from Price? Only to requisition by force. The result was that the Americans ceased to pay for transporting men and supplies from Montreal to Quebec. They had recourse to the simple expedient of forced labour. When Jean-Baptiste Badeaux, a notary at Trois Rivières, requested payment for the services rendered by the Ursuline Sisters who had attended the American sick and wounded, he was merely laughed at.[7] In these circumstances, those French Canadians who had once listened to the soft words of Congress, were now disposed to listen to the harsh words of *Civis Canadiensis* who had written, prophetically it would seem, in *The Quebec Gazette*, "These people to whom you have done no harm, come into your province to take your property with arms in their hands under a pretext of being your well-wishers, can you think, that these people who are without food and ammunition will allow you to enjoy peacefully the fruits of your labours, no; they will take your grain, your cattle and everything that you have (of which they have need) and they will pay you with notes; (which they call Province Bills, or Bills of Credit) what will you do with such money? nothing."[8]

On March 20th Wooster quitted Montreal to take command at Quebec. He was probably glad to go. He must have known that Simon Sanguinet was circulating an inflammatory letter to the French Canadians denouncing the "tyranny" the Americans had brought to the country, the new taxes to help pay for a war that the Americans had imposed on Canada, falling prices and forced labour. "Will you be more insensible than the beasts which, looking at their hurts, rouse themselves against those who have wounded them," he asked, urging Canadians to cease their secret mutterings and chase the "brigands" from the country.[9] It was couched in words familiar to the writers of manifestos at that time, and of all time. And Sanguinet was not alone. An anonymous paper was found posted on the church door in Trois Rivières telling the people to rise and sever the American line of communications between Quebec and Montreal. Such appeals were not, perhaps, too significant at that moment; but they were symptomatic of what was happening to the French Canadians, that more and more they were turning towards the idea of liberating their country from the unwelcome army that was occupying it. The Sieur de Beaujeu's rising in support of Carleton in the lower St. Lawrence, which led to the engagement at St. Pierre du Sud, was indicative of an attitude which was becoming widespread in French Canada. Hazen, who took over command in Montreal until the arrival of Arnold on April 19th, warned General Schuyler that the Canadians on whom they had counted so much were "no longer . . . friends, but on the contrary waiting an opportunity to join our enemies."[10] It was obvious even before the arrival of the expected British reinforcements in May, that the tide was turning in the political as well as in the military war.

The members of the Continental Congress had been always particularly sensitive to the importance of the political aspect of the invasion, and the news that was coming out of Canada was a source of growing alarm to them. They were, after all, as anxious to win the political war as the military war. Political victory was, in fact, the more important in the long run. This fact had been appreciated by Montgomery when the invasion force was being prepared, and both he and later Schuyler had asked that the troops might be accompanied by political commissioners who would take charge of the political conversion of the Canadians to the American point of view. Nothing, however, had been done at that time; but the idea was not dropped. After the military disaster at Quebec there were those Americans who felt that it was particularly important at this point not to abandon the task of political proselytization or let those adherents whom the Americans had already gained in the country lose heart. Both Hazen and a collaborator, Prudent Lajeunesse, made this point to the Continental Congress in Philadelphia in February. Finally, on February 15th, Congress resolved no longer to stand upon its dignity by insisting that the Canadians should come first to Philadelphia, but to appoint an American commission of three members which would make its way to Canada, counter the hostile and growing influence of the clergy among the habitants and restore faith in American ideas.

The leader of the group was Benjamin Franklin. Although now seventy years of age, he was chosen as the man who had, seventeen years previous, urged in London that Canada should be acquired by Great Britain and not be

Benjamin Franklin, an engraving by T. B. Welch from a portrait by Martin.

restored to France. His co-commissioners were to be two southerners, Samuel Chase and Charles Carroll, both of Maryland.[11] Although not officially appointed as commissioners, two others were attached to Franklin's party, namely, the Rev. John Carroll, a prominent Roman Catholic clergyman who was later to become first Catholic Archbishop of Baltimore, and Fleury Mesplet, a French printer of Philadelphia, who was to carry a printing press to Montreal and establish a newspaper there to provide a mouthpiece for the American point of view. The Rev. John Carroll, it was hoped, would be able to counter the influence of the French Canadian clergy, by persuading them of the "uprightness" of the American position and thereby to convince them to modify their opposition to the American rebellion and its representatives in Canada. To direct the commissioners in their task, Congress provided them with a letter of instructions, telling them to impress upon the Canadians the base, cruel and insidious designs of the British government in passing the Quebec Act, and the honest virtue of Congress in urging Canadians to adopt the principles of self-government. The commissioners were also to point out that the American invasion of Canada had no ulterior motive behind it, only the justifiable desire to frustrate British intentions to destroy "our common liberties" and to defeat the "hostile machinations" of Guy Carleton against the Thirteen Colonies. The Canadians were to be told that it was to their interests to become "inseparably united" with the other colonies. To remove their fears about the position of the church, the Canadians were to be assured that Congress would grant them the "free and undisturbed exercise of their religion." All of this was political propaganda. But in addition to their role as propagandists, the commissioners were expected to smooth out the areas of friction which had developed between the people of Canada and the troops of the occupying army, to encourage the resumption of the Indian trade and to ensure the acceptance of American currency by the local people.

A month's delay attended the departure of the three wise men while they awaited the drafting of these elaborate instructions. However, on April 2nd, Franklin and his companions set out. It was a long journey and a tiresome one, but finally the commissioners reached Montreal on April 29th. They were greeted by Arnold "in the most polite and friendly manner," taken to headquarters where "a genteel company of ladies and gentlemen had assembled" to welcome them, accorded a gun salute, and after supper taken to their lodgings in "the house of Mr. Thomas Walker, the best built and perhaps the best furnished house in this town." That is how Charles Carroll described it.[12]

The fact is that the Congress commission was a failure from the outset. It came too late, and the commissioners could do too little. Father Carroll made no headway among the French Canadian clergy, if only because he had no argument to answer the Canadian assertions that the Quebec Act had given the Catholic clergy all that they had hoped for and that the British had faithfully complied with and sanctioned the old laws of Canada. Even Carroll felt that "the judicious and liberal policy of the British Government to the Catholics had succeeded in inspiring them with sentiments of loyalty."[13] He therefore made no real effort to play the role of proselytizer, and made no converts to the American cause among the Canadian clergy; he failed to justify the hope expressed by General Lee that his presence in Canada would be worth several battalions to the American cause. Neither did Fleury Mesplet achieve very much. He set up his press in the Chateau de Ramezay but did not have a chance to bring out any publication. Events were moving too fast, and closing in upon the Americans.

Benjamin Franklin was the first commissioner to pack up and go home. His health had suffered from the hardships of the journey to Montreal, and he was astute enough to realize that a reaction had set in against the Americans and that there was little he could do to halt it. It had been expected that the commissioners would bring a large quantity of specie with them, but they had arrived empty-handed, and were able to do nothing but write to Congress about $14,000 owed by the Americans to Canadians, not to mention the monies owed to James Price. Franklin did, however, succeed in reversing the strict and arbitrary policy which had made Wooster so unpopular a figure in Montreal; arrests of suspected government supporters ceased, and militia officers lodged in the prisons of Fort Chambly were released and allowed to return home. But these acts of justice did not restore Canadian support; they only chagrined the "friends of liberty." The damage had been done. Finally, on May 11th, the dispirited Franklin and the disappointed Father Carroll left Montreal and began their return journey to the colonies to report to Congress at Philadelphia.

Whatever hopes the Americans now had of holding Canada rested wholly with the army. Clearly they were not going to hold it by popular support. Chase and Charles Carroll had left the political side of the mission entirely to Franklin and Father Carroll; they directed their attention to the military situation. Both men, therefore, left Montreal and went to Sorel where, on May 5th, they attended a council of war. Travelling through the "thickly seated" triangle formed by Montreal, Chambly and Sorel, they saw in it the most fertile land in the country and were convinced that it was essential, for strategic and economic reasons, that the Americans should defend it to the utmost. It was far too valuable to give up without a stiff fight. Both the commissioners and the army officers at Sorel realized that the arrival of British reinforcements would probably force a raising of the siege at Quebec, but they saw no reason to abandon the St. Lawrence. The best plan, they believed, would be to withdraw as far as Jacques Cartier, a strong position up the St. Lawrence from Quebec, fortify it, and meet the British at that point. This decision taken, Chase and Carroll then went to Chambly and St. Jean to examine the forts and the state of the garrisons. At St. Jean they found the fortifications only slightly damaged by the siege, although the buildings inside had been badly shaken up. The earthworks, however, seemed to be strong, and they concluded that St. Jean could soon be put into a good state of repair. At Chambly they expressed their wonder at Stopford's lethargic defence and speculated on why he had given up so readily. Then they returned to Montreal and on May 27th penned a report to Congress. Their work done, they set out for home, arriving at Ticonderoga on June 2nd.

The commissioners' letter of May 27th made melancholy reading in Philadelphia. Everywhere they had gone they found nothing but confusion, lack of discipline, shortages of tents, meat, bread, shoes and clothing, and soldiers sick, disgruntled, unpaid and mutinous. Short term enlistments had failed to produce an army possessing any cohesion or spirit. The credit of Congress was exhausted and even a cart was not to be found "without ready money or force." The logistical side of the campaign had completely collapsed, and the commissioners were so afraid that the troops would mutiny for lack of provisions that they agreed that American officers were justified in requisitioning supplies by force to keep the men from engaging in general plunder on their own. "We cannot find words strong enough to express our miserable situation," they wrote, "you will have a faint idea of it, if you figure to yourselves an army broken and dishearted, half of it under inoculation or other diseases; soldiers without pay, without discipline, and altogether reduced to live from hand to mouth, depending on the scanty and precarious supplies of a few half starved cattle and trifling quantities of flour, which have hitherto been picked up in different parts of the country."

For this deplorable situation Wooster, the commissioners believed, had to bear full responsibility. As they saw him, "General Wooster is . . . unfit, totally unfit, to command your Army and conduct the war. . . . His stay in this Colony is unnecessary and even prejudicial to our affairs; we would therefore humbly advise his recall."[14]

But even the disappearance of Wooster was not going to save the Americans in Canada. By this time Carleton's troops were beginning to move in upon them, both from the west and from the east.

II. The American defeat at the Cedars

During the winter of 1775-1776, while Carleton was undergoing siege at Quebec, small British garrisons, consisting of detachments of men from the 8th (The King's Regiment), had remained undisturbed in the various western posts extending from Oswegatchie to Michillimackinac. To these posts, and in particular to Niagara, there was a steady movement of Indians, if only to participate in the expected hand-outs of food and drink. Both were distributed by the post commanders, together with many exhortations not to take up arms but to "support the king's peace." Then, in the spring, anticipating that Colonel Guy Johnson and Joseph Brant would be returning from England, bands of Cayuga, Seneca and Mississauga Indians set off down the St. Lawrence in the direction of Montreal. These Indians arrived at Oswegatchie and supplied the commander, Captain George Forster, with the basic force he required to undertake any operations of an offensive nature against the left flank of the American position in Canada.

The Americans had made no attempt during the winter of 1775-1776 to molest Forster, perhaps because his post was too insignificant to justify the mounting of an operation when every man was needed for the far more important attack upon Quebec; perhaps, too, because they realized that should Quebec fall to Montgomery's assault, there would be nothing that Forster could do but surrender on demand. Certainly Oswegatchie was a post of no great military strength, although it did offer a potential jumping-off place for any attack which might be contemplated against Montreal by the garrisons and Indians of the west.

But if the west was regarded as of little consequence by the politicians in Philadelphia or by the commander of the northern army in his office at Albany, it was of the greatest importance to the merchants of Montreal. The western Indian trade had been the life-blood of New France during the Ancien Régime, and it had been the Indian trade which, because of the opportunities it afforded for the accumulation of wealth, induced many of the American merchants to leave their homes in the colonies and make their way to Montreal. Although a number of these merchants had given their support, real and moral, to Montgomery and the invading army, they did not find the American military authorities sympathetic to their desire to re-open the Indian trade. One of the terms which the citizenry had presented to

Montgomery, when he accepted the surrender of Montreal, was that the Indian trade should be carried on "as freely as heretofore," and that passports should be granted "for that purpose."[15] But this was just what Wooster was not prepared to do. American military officers realized that, with the exception of the Caughnawaga, the Indians generally were tied to the British, and they suspected that any opening of the trade would simply play into enemy hands by affording opportunities to British agents to renew contacts with the Indians with a view to encouraging them to take up the hatchet. General Wooster's orders were precise; he would "suffer the Merchants of Montreal to send none of their woolen Cloths out of the town."[16] This was not what the merchants had bargained for. Instead of giving them a free hand economically, the Americans were placing restrictions upon their activities. The result was the only petition that was sent out of Montreal to the Continental Congress, when a group of merchants, early in February, begged Congress to permit the granting of passports to the west and the re-opening of the trade. Herein lies the explanation of why Wooster reported to his superiors that the merchants were not, as he had hoped, disposed to assist him if they could avoid it, and why Hazen wrote to Schuyler on April 1st that, "With respect to the better sort of people, both French and English, seven-eights are Tories who would wish to see our throats cut, and perhaps would readily assist in doing it."[17] When Franklin, Chase and Carroll arrived, they saw at once the political significance of what was happening in Montreal as a result of Wooster's refusal to permit any contact with the western Indians, and began to issue the passes demanded. Thomas Walker was astute enough to see what might occur once this were done, but Franklin and the others hoped that their conciliatory gesture would be an incentive to gratitude. What they did not realize was that it came, as conciliatory gestures so often do, too late to be of an advantage to the authority making it.

This action, together with the knowledge that several well known supporters of the government, Stanley Goddard, Richard Walker and the Chevalier de Lorimier had slipped out of Montreal surreptitiously, gave cause for alarm among the military officers at Montreal. And when rumours that a force of Indians, Canadians and regulars was planning to descend the St. Lawrence began to circulate in Montreal late in April, Benedict Arnold, now in command of the city, ordered Colonel Timothy Bedel to take up a position some forty miles above Montreal in order "to prevent any goods being sent to the upper country, and to guard against a surprise from the enemy or other Indians."[18] Bedel took with him 390 men from the New Hampshire and Connecticut regiments lately arrived in Canada as reinforcements for the army on the St. Lawrence, and two pieces of artillery, and entrenched himself behind a wooden stockade at a post known as the Cedars, located on the St. Lawrence at the second rapid between Lake Francis and Lake St. Louis.

Forster had kept himself informed during the winter, by means of his Indian spies, of what was going on in Montreal, and knew of Bedel's move to the Cedars. And what gaps there were in his knowledge were filled in by Lorimier after his escape from Montreal. Lorimier had visited some of the western Indians as far west as Gananoque and had brought some of them to Oswegatchie. Forster therefore assembled a small strike-force, comprising several officers and 36 rank and file of the 8th Regiment, 11 British and Canadian volunteers and about 160 Indians from various tribes.[19] On May 12th he began his descent of the St. Lawrence in the direction of Montreal. Two days later he picked up an additional group of 54 Indians from the mission post at St. Regis and then pushed on to the west end of Lake St. Francis where he gained further intelligence of the nature and strength of Bedel's force. There was some hesitancy on the part of the Indians when they discovered that the Americans numbered almost 400 men; however, when an express arrived from Carleton with news that British regular troops had landed at Quebec and that the Americans were on the run, the Indians were elated and showed "great spirit" in their willingness to proceed with the expedition. Meanwhile Lorimier, who was in charge of them, had gone to the Catholic mission at the Cedars to get in touch with the local priest, Rev. Pierre Denaut, who later became Bishop of Quebec, and a merchant named Denis, in order to arrange for provisions for Forster's force. Despite the fact that he was disguised as an Indian, Lorimier very narrowly escaped detection by an American patrol. Then, on May 18th, Forster's force disembarked from their canoes about three miles from Bedel's post and prepared to attack.

Bedel, too, had his Indian spies, and Forster's approach was no secret to him. But instead of endeavouring to organize a proper resistance, he pleaded illness, turned his responsibilities over to his second in command, Major Isaac Butterfield, and hastened to Montreal to spread the news of the British attack. When his report reached Arnold who was, at that moment, at Sorel, the American commander immediately detached 150 men and ordered Major Henry Sherburn to hurry them to Butterfield's relief. Meanwhile Arnold himself undertook to assemble more men and follow Sherburn to the Cedars. Sherburn left Montreal on the 17th. However, owing to the difficulty of getting adequate transport to convey his men up Lake St. Louis, it was not until May 18th that he succeeded in reaching a landing point about nine miles from his objective.

During this time Forster's men had taken their positions in front of the American fort at the Cedars. Lacking cannon, Forster could not batter down its feeble wooden walls, and both sides limited their fighting to an exchange of musket shots at distances often beyond range, without making much impression on each other. Butterfield, it would seem, was terrified, as were many of his men, more by the shouts and screams of the Indians than by their muskets, fearing for his life should he fall into their hands. He would not let his men sally out of the stockade and Forster had no means of forcing him to do so. Forster therefore sent out a drum and a flag of truce demanding the surrender of the fort while it was still in his hands to save the lives of the American soldiers before the Indians had suffered any extensive casualties. A counter-demand by the Americans that they be allowed to take their arms with them was rejected and the shooting began again. The next day Forster was joined by a small group of Canadians under Jean Baptiste Louvigny, Sieur de Montigny, a fur trader who had been with Belestre at St. Jean, and Lormier proposed that the British and Indians carry out an assault of the fort from two sides simultaneously. At this point news arrived of Sherburn's approach. Montigny was, therefore, detached to keep a watch on his progress.

Unaware that help was near, Butterfield finally sent word to Forster offering his surrender if the lives of his men could be secured from the Indians. Forster was anxious to accept it. He replied to Butterfield that he had "by entreaty, overcome the resolutions formed by the Savages, of allowing no quarter, on your refusing my offer to you, and am happy to assure you and your garrison personal safety."[20] The Americans were then marched out of the fort while the Indians were allowed the plunder, "which belonged to them," inside the fort. When the Indians had satisfied themselves, the prisoners were returned to the barracks in the fort. Despite the fact that the prisoners had been promised nothing more than "the cloaths on their backs," the Americans had made up their packs to carry with them. Forster was concerned about this action. He knew that it would "discontent" the Indians, but felt satisfied when, with the assistance of two chiefs he was able to restrain the Indians from taking more than a few minor articles. The British officers felt that the Americans had come out of what might have developed into a dangerous situation reasonably well, with only the loss of some watches, money and "a laced hat or two." Writing of this episode, Captain Andrew Parke of the 8th observed, "We do verily believe" that the Indians took nothing else, "nor did they (the prisoners) receive any insult."[21]

Meanwhile, Sherburn, having landed his men several miles from the Cedars on the 18th, sent a scout ahead to learn what was happening there. The news that the American commander received was grossly exaggerated — he was told that the British and Indians with a force of 500 men were marching to attack him — but accepting it as the truth, he hurriedly re-embarked and paddled back to Fort Anne on Montreal island. Early the next morning he discovered to his surprise that Butterfield was still holding out and once more he set off for the Cedars. This time the Indians were waiting for him. Suddenly, as the Americans were about four miles from their destination, they were attacked by Lorimier's Indians and later by Montigny's Canadians. The engagement was short and sharp. The Americans fought well but believed themselves, mistakenly, to be outnumbered, and

Sherburn capitulated without any stipulation. He yielded to Lorimier with 97 of his men, having suffered only minor casualties.[22] Lorimier's losses had also been comparatively light, although one of them had been an important Seneca war chief, whose death aroused the anger of the Indians and their desire for revenge. Despite the efforts of Forster's officers, they began threatening the prisoners. Whether any member of Sherburn's party really was killed by Indians after the surrender is a matter of historical dispute, but there does seem to have been a certain amount of jostling and looting on the part of Indians who claimed that, by Indian custom, prisoners were the individual property of their captors. For this reason some of the Indians refused to give up their captives, even to Forster. There is, however, no dispute about the number of men who surrendered; when they were marched back to the Cedars and added to those already in the barracks, they totalled no fewer than 487.[23]

After sending the rebel officers on parole to be looked after by the priests at Lake of Two Mountains,[24] Forster set out with his men and the rest of the prisoners for Montreal Island on May 21st. At Fort Senneville — a property belonging to Montigny — he established a camp. Then, on the 24th, he advanced eastwards as far as Pointe Claire, where he had been told a number of Canadians were ready to join his ranks. Here, about 18 miles from Montreal, his force numbered in the vicinity of 500 men, including troops, Canadians and Indians. Continuing his advance he came within 3 miles of Lachine. At this point his scouts reported that Arnold had returned to Montreal from Sorel, gathered a substantial relief force including most of the Montreal garrison, and was waiting for him entrenched with cannon in a stone house at Lachine. Arnold commanded a force amounting to probably 600 men; but with the arrival of the various garrisons from the outposts around Montreal, and the rapid approach of Colonel De Haas's regiment of Pennsylvanians from Sorel, he was counting on a defending force of something in the nature of 1500 men.

By this time Forster's little army was beginning to diminish in numbers. The Indians were never a constant or reliable force, each man being free to choose if and when he should return home. As groups of Indians began to leave the Montreal region for reasons which were satisfactory to themselves, Forster realized that he was becoming weaker at the very moment Arnold was growing stronger. Hearing no word of any British movement up the St. Lawrence from Quebec, he believed that he had no choice but to pull back, first to Pointe Claire and then to the Cedars. At this latter point Forster, embarrassed by the numbers of his prisoners, decided to act upon a suggestion already put forward by some American officers, namely, to arrange a mutual exchange of prisoners with the Americans. He accordingly sent Captain Andrew Parke to Two Mountains to discuss the matter with the officers of the Congress army. The Americans were scarcely anxious to remain with their unruly captors and the prospect of returning to the colonies was an alluring one. They therefore raised no obstacles to an agreement to exchange prisoners on a man for man, rank for rank basis. They even accepted the insertion in the terms of the "cartel" of a restriction forbidding them to take up arms again against the British for the duration of the war, an obligation which was not to be placed upon the British prisoners when they should be released. The Americans, however, were to be provided with bateaux for their return journey, during which they agreed not to commit "any waste or spoil," and to return the bateaux to the British. Prisoners from both sides were to give undertakings not to reveal any military secrets to which they might have become privy as a result of their capture. The "cartel" was signed by Parke, Montigny and Lorimier on behalf of Forster, and by Butterfield and Sherburn, and several of the American junior officers. Those involved in the exchange included 2 majors, 9 captains, 21 subalterns, 4 hostages, 8 Canadians (released), 8 men bought from the Indians and 2 still to be purchased, and 443 privates, or a total of 497. There were to be four hostages of the rank of captain who would remain with the British as a guarantee of the faithful execution of the cartel by the enemy.

Learning of Forster's withdrawal, Arnold plunged aggressively ahead to reach Fort Anne at the east end of Montreal Island. The next day, May 26th, the day of the signing of the cartel, he embarked in bateaux and proceeded towards Vaudreuil, where he could discern Forster's men waiting for him in battle formation. Arnold, however, did not choose to land at that point. He preferred to keep his bateaux beyond the range of the British and Indian muskets, and when Forster opened fire with the two cannon he had taken from the Americans at the Cedars, the American commander allowed his bateaux to drift out of reach of the British guns. He was tactician enough not to try a frontal attack from unprotected bateaux when a few well placed cannon balls might send his boats and his men to the river bottom before he could even get within musket range of the shore. Wisely avoiding a daylight attack, Arnold began to think in terms of crossing the river at night, moving through the woods and striking his opponent on the flank and in the rear in the early hours of dawn. Discussing this plan with his officers, he was both surprised and annoyed to find that most of them were sceptical of its advantages. They took the view that, owing to the alertness of the Indians, a surprise was unlikely, and that they might themselves get caught in the confusion of a night manoeuvre and suffer a serious reverse. The discussion went on for some time and it was after midnight when the council of war broke up in a flurry of sharp words between Arnold the hawk, and Hazen the dove.

Two hours later Captain Parke and Major Sherburn arrived at the American camp under a flag of truce. Sherburn had seen how Forster's Indians had reacted when they heard Arnold's threat that if they offered any resistance to an American attack he would burn every Indian town he came across and kill every Indian who fell into his hands. According to Sherburn, the Indians replied that they would kill every prisoner in their hands the moment Arnold launched his attack. He knew they were serious and that such an action would not be out of keeping with their practice. He therefore urged Arnold to adhere to the cartel he and Butterfield and the other American officers had accepted. It would be the only way to save the lives of the Americans in the British camp. Arnold was caught and he knew it. In his own account he wrote, "I was torn by the conflicting passions of revenge and humanity . . . a sufficient force to take ample revenge raging for action, urged me on the one hand, and humanity for five hundred unhappy wretches, who were upon the point of being sacrificed if our vengeance was not delayed, plead equally strong on the other."[25] Humanity won out and after persuading Forster to expunge the section requiring the Americans to refrain from serving again during the war, he signed the cartel. Nobody said anything about any alleged ill-treatment suffered by the American prisoners.

In the evening of the same day, May 27th, the first bateaux carrying Forster's American prisoners left Vaudreuil for Fort Anne. Owing, however, to high winds and the dangers of sailing these rather clumsy craft in rough waters, the transfer of the prisoners was not concluded until May 30th. Forster then retired to Oswegatchie. Arnold had already departed for Montreal, leaving De Haas to look after the details of caring for the prisoners. Then De Haas too retired as far as Lachine. With him he still had in his pocket an order signed by Arnold commanding him to burn the Indian village of Conosadaga, but, after consulting his officers, he decided to ignore it. Such an action would have served no useful military purpose and might, on the contrary, have aroused the Indians to revengeful reprisals of a kind with which De Haas had no desire to cope.[26] The American prisoners were now happily on their way to the colonies. But the politicians in Philadelphia, far from the scene of the cartel, were incensed at what Butterfield and Arnold had done. They would not concede to either officer the right to enter into any such agreement with the British and argued that, in any case, the cartel had been violated by the Indians who had killed and pillaged their prisoners. When the hostage, Captain Ebenezer Sullivan, wrote in July, giving the lie to the charges of callous brutality levelled against Forster,[27] his voice was lost in the increasing volume of atrocity stories which circulated throughout the colonies and were magnified by their repeated telling.

III. Carleton's Victory at Trois Rivières and the American Retreat to the Frontier

If Forster's western offensive towards Montreal failed to achieve anything more than a local tactical success, it was because Carleton's thrust from Quebec was not carried through simultaneously with expedition and despatch. Co-ordination of the two movements was essential for complete success. But it is doubtful if Carleton ever thought in terms of, or deliberately planned, a co-ordinated offensive. He was satisfied, for the moment, to ensure that there were no more enemy soldiers within the immediate vicinity of Quebec and no more traitors within the city. Accordingly he was content to allow the Americans to remain at Deschambault, now that he had chased them away from Quebec, and to concentrate upon the problems presented by the English and French Canadian collaborators. He was determined to prevent the re-entry into the city of those who had left it because they were unwilling to do militia service or because they felt that the Americans would be the winning side. Accordingly, on May 12th, he issued a proclamation forbidding any "Person or Persons ... who quitted the City of Quebec" as a consequence of his proclamation of November 22nd, or who "deserted or withdrew from any corps to which they once belonged," to "presume to enter the said City again without a Permission in writing under my Hand or under Hand of the Lieutenant-governor of this Province."[28] This proclamation Carleton followed by appointing a commission to look into the nature and extent of Canadian collaboration with the enemy during the previous autumn and winter months. As members of the commission he named François Baby, Gabriel Taschereau and Jenkin Williams. Between May 22nd and July 16th the commissioners visited the various parishes north and south of the St. Lawrence between Trois Rivières and Kamouraska, assembling the militia, cancelling American commissions, withdrawing royal commissions from unreliable militia officers, appointing new and loyal officers, and obtaining the names of those who not only gave active assistance to the enemy but who arrested loyalists and imposed their will upon the silent and neutral majority. The commissioners went about their task thoroughly and not unfairly, and their report revealed that while there had been strong active groups of rebel sympathisers along the south shore, particularly in Pointe de Lévis, Saint Vallier, the Island of Orleans and St. Pierre du Sud, there had also been few French Canadians in the parishes abutting on Quebec, such as Ancienne Lorette, Jeune Lorette and Charlesbourg, who had thrown in their lot with the American rebels. If anything, the report emphasized the strong desire for neutrality which had existed throughout the country. Left to themselves, the majority of the French Canadians would have been non-participants in the events of 1775-1776. A similar commission was subsequently appointed for the Montreal district, which included St. George Dupré, Pierre· Panet and William Gray. This latter body, however, did not function until after Carleton had re-occupied the city with an army at his back.

Carleton always believed in the ultimate good will of the French Canadian population towards himself and the policy which he hoped to establish in Canada by means of the Quebec Act. The fact that the French Canadian habitants had not sprung to arms in his defence, he was inclined to attribute to the machinations of ill-disposed English merchants and the insidious propaganda of the agents of Congress. The same simple approach to politics can be discerned in his attitude towards the American soldiers whom he encountered during the course of the war. They too were just "deluded subjects" who had been misled by self-interested demagogues like Samuel Adams. Treat them with kindness and they would return to their sense of duty and allegiance. Herein lies the explanation of Carleton's policy towards the Americans during the year 1776. His first action was to send out patrols to find the stragglers, the fugitives, the sick and the wounded who, fearing death at the hands of the victors, might die unattended in the woods, or in the barn of some not too sympathetic habitant. This he followed up by a proclamation ordering all captains of militia to make a diligent search for those poor wretched people who were "in great danger of perishing for want of proper assistance" and to assure them that "as soon as their health is restored" they would have "free liberty to return to their respective provinces."[29] When Morgan and some of the officers who had been taken on December 31st petitioned Carleton for permission to return home "on parole," the governor readily granted their request, "Since we have tried in vain to make them acknowledge us as brothers," he is said to have remarked, "let us send them away, disposed to regard us as first cousins."[30] To each of the men Carleton gave a much needed shirt and some money. Morgan later reported that the treatment accorded the prisoners while they were in British hands had been a mixture of kindly consideration on the part of Carleton and constant coldheartedness on the part of the guards.

However Carleton may have seen his policy, Maclean saw it differently. He feared that Carleton's delays and softness would lose him the campaign. There was nothing of the milksop about the outspoken Scot. He saw no reason why the enemy should be given any opportunity to recover from "the Panick and Consternation" to which "their late Precipitate retreat from Quebec has reduced them." One can read between the lines of a letter he wrote on May 10th his criticism of his senior officer: "I . . . hope we have had Experience Sufficient to convince us that our Unactivity and want of Spirit was what greatly contributed to the distresses to which this province has been reduced last year, timidity in the field My Lord is a dangerous matter, for I am convinced few Generals are capable of conducting a defensive War."[31] Carleton may not have been guilty of timidity but he was guilty of "unactivity," at least in the sense Maclean understood it. Except the recovery of *Gaspé* by the Navy, Carleton engaged in no military activity until May 22nd, when he set off with several ships bearing the 47th and 29th Regiments for Trois Rivières. Maclean may well have hoped that he would be in charge of this expedition. But Carleton had kept it for himself, and although he learned of Forster's success at the Cedars, instead of pushing ahead he chose at that moment to hurry back to Quebec to welcome General Burgoyne who arrived at Quebec on June 1st, with seven British regiments from Ireland, four batteries of artillery, several regiments of Brunswick troops commanded by General Riedesel, and a substantial military chest. At least Carleton's absence gave Maclean temporary command of the British force at Trois Rivières, and the "Beloved, Dreaded and Indefatigable" Highlander, as a British naval officer described him,[32] began landing troops and setting up camp pending Carleton's return.

General David Wooster, whose administration of Montreal had brought down upon his head the wrath of the commissioners of Congress, had taken over command of the American troops before Quebec at the beginning of April. Just one month later, on May 1st, he was superseded by Major General John Thomas. Thomas had not been pleased with the condition of the American army as he had seen it on his way to Quebec, and on May 5th he proposed, at a council of war, that the army should be withdrawn from Quebec to fortified positions farther up the St. Lawrence at Jacques Cartier and Deschambault. The arrival, the following day, May 6th, of British vessels bearing reinforcements for Carleton caught Thomas by surprise and forced a precipitate and ignominious retreat where an orderly withdrawal had been his hope. Since Thomas had had no chance to erect works of any kind at Jacques Cartier, the retreating army tried to put as much distance as it could between itself and the British, and spread confusion and smallpox all along the St. Lawrence as far as Deschambault. Here a halt was made on May 7th, and during the hours that followed, stragglers in every condition of despair and exhaustion stumbled and shuffled into the village. They had had no easy time of it, for British vessels had followed their retreat, hurling shells into every concentration of troops within range.

Deschambault offered the Americans certain advantages from the standpoint of defence, but, although Thomas was anxious to make a stand at this point, his officers and men were not. Only Edward Antill was inclined to stay, but he was so heavily compromised that he had no choice but to follow the Americans wherever they might go. The fact was that the American army was in no shape to withstand a strong attack, and it was, in any event, likely to be outflanked by the superior mobility which command of the river gave to Carleton. Thomas had to rest content with a rear guard at Deschambault while ordering the main body of his army to continue their withdrawal to Sorel. And shortly afterwards even the rear guard was withdrawn on the general's orders.

It was May 17th or 18th when Thomas reached Sorel. On the 21st he met the commissioners from Congress and on the same day contracted smallpox. For Thomas it was the smallpox which was the more fatal of the two scourges, for, by June 2nd, he was dead. The commissioners, however, did no more harm than ignore the normal channels of military command and insist, without an adequate appreciation of the situation, upon the return of American troops to Deschambault. They accepted too readily the rumours circulating throughout the American camp that Carleton's reinforcements consisted only of a couple of regiments from Halifax, and that the British commander's reluctance to engage in an active pursuit sprang from the fact that he was not strong enough to carry out a major operation. It was therefore the commissioners who were responsible for John Sullivan, Thomas's successor, ordering his troops back down the river, an order which was greeted with little enthusiasm by the American soldiers, but which was joyfully received by men like Duggan and some of the Canadians still committed to the American cause. A report that Maclean's force at Trois Rivières numbered only 300 men spurred the Americans into action. There would be no problem in disposing of a force as small as that. Sullivan exuded confidence from every pore. "I venture to assure you and the Congress," he wrote to Washington from Sorel, "that I can, in a few days, reduce the army to order, and with the assistance of a kind Providence, put a new face to our affairs here, which a few days since seemed almost impossible. The enemy's ships are now above Deschambault, and if General Thompson succeeds at Trois Rivières, I will soon remove the ships below Richelieu Falls (Deschambault) and after that, approach Quebec as fast as possible."[33]

What Sullivan did not know when he wrote that letter was that additional vessels and British troops had reached Quebec, and that Carleton, unaware of any impending American operation, had sent Lieutenant Colonel Simon Fraser of the 24th Regiment of Foot up the river with four battalions of regulars to take post at Trois Rivières, and in his wake another brigade of regulars under Lieutenant Colonel William Nesbitt of the 47th,[34] protected by the sloop-of-war, *Martin*, Fraser landed to join forces with Maclean; Nesbitt's men remained on board the transports anchored in the river. Neither did Sullivan know that when the British troops landed, they were greeted with a salute of three volleys of musket fire by the local militia and shouts of "Vive le Roy."[35] Thus all of the information on which Sullivan had undertaken to reverse the American movement and send men back towards Quebec was both false and misleading.

Completely ignorant of the fact that his opponents had been considerably reinforced, Brigadier General William Thompson set out from Sorel on the afternoon of June 6th with a force of some 2000 men. Travelling by boat, he moved along the south shore of Lac St. Pierre as far as Nicolet and then, under cover of the darkness on June 7th, he crossed the lake to Pointe du Lac, about seven miles up river from Trois Rivières. Leaving 250 men at Pointe du Lac to guard the boats, Thompson set out on foot. He did not know the country and obtained the assistance of a local farmer, Antoine Gautier by name, who acted as guide. Dividing his troops up into several columns Thompson began to push slowly forward, travelling through the woods out of sight of the river. Gautier, however, was not to be relied upon. He deliberately misled Thompson's column into a heavy morass which, as the Americans struggled onwards, seemed to grow deeper and more impenetrable. Up to the waists in slime, tripping over half submerged logs, the American soldiers strove to get back to the river road, only to find

Brigadier-General Simon Fraser who commanded one of Burgoyne's brigades in Canada in 1776. He was killed during the British counter-invasion of New York in 1777.

Martin and other British vessels ready to open fire upon them with cannon. Forced back into the bog, they had no choice but to flounder through it as best they could. Travelling by a different route, some of the other troops managed to work their way through the heavy undergrowth, but upon reaching open ground found themselves directly opposite Fraser's soldiers, drawn up in battle formation. A local militiaman, Captain Landron, had seen the Americans land at Pointe du Lac and had hastened to send warning to Fraser.[36] There was some fighting, but the advantages were all with the British, and when field pieces were brought up to sweep the woods the Americans broke and fled, pursued by the grenadiers and light infantry companies of the 9th, 20th and 62nd Regiments. Those Americans who did not give themselves up or submit to capture sought safety in the dark recesses of the forest. At Trois Rivières the Americans lost some twenty-five or more killed and probably as many wounded; more serious in terms of numbers was the loss of 200 prisoners, including General Thompson, his second in command, William Irvine, and sixteen other officers.[37] The men at Pointe du Lac took to the boats as soon as news arrived of the American defeat, and the scattered fragments of Thompson's ill-starred force were compelled to struggle all the way back to Berthier on foot, individually and in small groups, and then to cross the St. Lawrence to find refuge in Sorel. Meanwhile the prisoners were sent back to Quebec where, on August 6th, Carleton released them all and provided them with comfortable passage back to New York. The "Musketoes of a Monsterous size and innumerable numbers" had been harder on the Americans than the British general.[38] A British officer who witnessed the events of June 8th at Trois Rivières wrote later, "the Surprize the Rebels felt at finding us so prepared to receive them, contrary to their Expectations, and the Alertness and Steadyness of the King's Troops on the Occasion, I believe occasioned their precipitate Flight Thro' the Province, for they never after dared shew a Countenance, tho' in some places strongly Intrenched, particularly at Sorrel. . . ."[39]

It is astonishing to the modern soldier that Carleton failed to take full advantage of the victory he had gained on June 8th. Instead of allowing Fraser's men to push rapidly ahead to intercept the stragglers and block their escape to Sorel, Carleton held Fraser in leash, an action which led both Berthelot at Trois Rivières and Sanguinet, who had left Montreal to join Carleton in Quebec, to suggest that the British commander actually wanted the demoralized remnants of Thompson's corps to escape to Sorel.[40] It may be that Carleton was unaware of the real weakness in numbers and morale of the American forces under Sullivan. But with 8000 men, including those who had arrived under Burgoyne and Riedesel, what had he to fear?

On June 9th the British troops were all ordered aboard the several vessels, with the exception of Fraser's corps of 1200 men, who were to march along the north shore of the river. But there was no forward movement until June 14th when Carleton arrived to take command of the armada. A contemporary participant described the advance in his diary. "About One o'clock in the Morning, his Excellency General Carleton came up, and order'd the Fleet to get under Way, the Wind then blowing fair; but soon after being alarmed by some Firing on Shore, was again order'd to come to an anchor. In less than an Hour the General's Ship got under Way, sailed ahead towards the Frigate, when the whole Fleet weighed, and at Day light was ordered to form a line, as well as the Channel would admit. The object was the finest I ever beheld; upwards of Eighty Sail, with near 8000 Troops on Board, appeared like a moving Forest."[41] Towards evening the fleet reached Sorel where instructions were issued to the troops to hold themselves in readiness to disembark. The grenadiers and the light infantry landed first, followed by the battalions of Nesbitt's division. The Americans offered no resistance. They had, in fact, abandoned their lines that very morning about 10 A.M., and were pressing their way up the Richelieu towards Chambly and St. Jean. Nesbitt, however, took no chances; his troops took post as they landed and lay all night on their arms.

At first Sullivan had thought seriously of trying to hold Sorel. A self-made man — he had risen from stable boy to major general — he had plenty of confidence in himself. He was aware of the strong desire expressed by Congress to retain a foothold on the St. Lawrence, and, although a large proportion of his army was down with sickness, he was still able to muster 2500 effectives, including 424 New Englanders, 681 troops from New Jersey, 1361 Pennsylvania infantry and four companies of artillery.[42] And not too far away were strong detachments in Montreal, Berthier, Chambly and St. Jean. Brown had intimidated Prescott into surrender with far fewer

men than that. But in November 1775 the Americans had been filled with
the zeal and confidence born of success on the field of battle; Sullivan's men
were broken in spirit by sickness and defeat. The American general had tried
the time-honoured military method of restoring discipline and a sense of
pride in each soldier by issuing the order on June 11th, "Every non-
commissioned officer or soldier who shall come to the parade dirty, with a
long beard, or his breeches-knees open, shall be mulcted of a day's allowance
of provisions, and do a double tour of duty."[43] He had tried, too, to keep his
men busy by ordering the construction of earthworks and battery positions
at Berthier. But his army was slowly bleeding to death from desertions, and
when Sullivan and his officers learned that Carleton's fleet had entered Lac
St. Pierre, they decided to pull out as quickly as possible. The Richelieu
River pointed the road which led to Lake Champlain and home. On the
morning of June 14th the retreat began. It was not a rout. The baggage and
ordnance were placed on board the available water craft, and with the
exception of several guns too large to manhandle over the Richelieu rapids,
not a weapon or an entrenching tool was left behind. By 9 o'clock the next
evening Sullivan's men, fatigued beyond description, found what shelter they
could from the rain at Chambly and tried to snatch a few hours' rest before
taking up the march again. The detachment at Berthier had not been warned
of the retreat. It was cut off by Carleton's fleet and made its way on foot to
Montreal to join Arnold.

At Sorel, Carleton divided his army. One division was placed under
Lieutenant General Burgoyne, who was given the task of pursuing Sullivan's
retreating rebels. On the morning of the 15th, Burgoyne went ashore with
the 9th and 31st Regiments and with an army numbering about 4000 men
and six 6 pounder guns. He placed his light infantry and the Canadians, who
were coming in daily in greater numbers to support the victorious
government forces, in the van and on the flanks, and followed behind with
the grenadiers, the artillery and the battalions of the line, in that order. But
Burgoyne was, owing to Carleton's dilatory tactics at Trois Rivières, a full
twenty-four hours behind his quarry. The second division remained under
Carleton himself, who, with the fleet, continued up the St. Lawrence
towards Arnold's base, Montreal. With a little luck he might have been able
to catch the American completely by surprise.

In Montreal, Benedict Arnold, having returned to the city after his deal
with Forster, was uneasy about the absence of information from Sullivan.
Finally, on June 15th, he decided to send his aide, Captain James Wilkinson,
with despatches addressed to Sullivan whom he still believed to be at Sorel.
Wilkinson, travelling by canoe down the St. Lawrence, almost bumped into
Carleton's fleet, windbound, near Varennes. He escaped ashore, stole a horse,
and galloped back to Longueuil to send his news to his astonished
commander in the Chateau de Ramezay. Arnold never moved faster. Within
four hours his troops had evacuated Montreal, first failing in an attempt to

General John Burgoyne who commanded the British troops who relieved Quebec and drove the Americans out of Canada during 1776.

burn the city before their departure. As soon as the flames were extinguished by the local citizens, the superior of St. Sulpice, Monsieur Montgolfier, turned the keys of the city over to Colonel Dufy-Desaunier. The militia was then assembled, and militiamen patrolled the streets and guarded the gates until the arrival of the royal troops on June 17th.

Fearing lest he be overtaken by the British, Arnold sent Wilkinson to Chambly to obtain help from Sullivan. Meanwhile he started marching his men to Laprairie on the road to St. Jean. Wilkinson reached the Richelieu and was appalled by what he saw, "The front of our retreating army, overwhelmed with fatigue, lay scattered in disorder over the plain, and buried deep in sleep, without a single sentinel to watch for its safety."[44] To add to the confusion of the moment, the commander of the rear guard, Brigadier General the Baron De Woedtke, was "drunk, and in front of the enemy,"[45] and it was only after he found Colonel Anthony Wayne that Wilkinson was able to get any help at all. However, by the time Wayne's men were mustered, Arnold was well on the road to safety, burning his bridges behind him. At Chambly Sullivan finally managed to get the army moving again on the morning of the 16th. Burning the fort and the sawmills of the neighbourhood and all row galleys and other water craft they could not use, the Americans dragged themselves slowly towards St. Jean. Here, on June 17th, Sullivan joined forces with Arnold and his troops from Montreal. While several thousand disheartened American soldiers huddled in the swamps, Sullivan and Arnold and the other officers discussed the next step to be taken. There was, however, little choice and no real argument in favour of trying to hold the fort, and the decision was unanimous to continue the retreat to Crown Point. The dead were thrown into pits, the wounded and sick placed on the boats, and the miserable army set out once again.

Only one boat stayed at St. Jean. That was Arnold's. Even if he was not prepared to fight a useless battle for a useless fortification, Arnold had lost none of his swagger. With Wilkinson he set out on horseback to reconnoitre the road to Chambly. Catching sight of Burgoyne's advance guard, the two men returned at a gallop to St. Jean where, on Arnold's orders, they shot their horses – Wilkinson doing so with even greater reluctance than Hazen had showed when he set the torch to his own house near St. Jean – and Arnold, resisting all proffers of assistance, pushed off the boat with his own hands,[45] thus indulging, said Wilkinson, "the vanity of being the last man who embarked from the shores of the enemy." He had already sent to Albany a quantity of requisitioned merchandise which would enable him to indulge other fancies than his taste for the dramatic.[46] Hard on Arnold's heels came Burgoyne's Canadian volunteers and light infantry, but all they captured was a single Indian, setting fire to a bridge between the two redoubts. Wrote one of the officers of Burgoyne's force, "The last Rebel Boat turned the Corner of the Wood just as Captn. Craig's party arrived at the Fort."[47] Burgoyne had made up most of his twenty-four hour handicap, but, like Carleton at Montreal, he had just failed to catch the retreating Americans. Wilkinson found it hard to understand why the British had not put forward that little extra effort which would have insured complete victory. In his *Memoirs* he remarked, "When these last scenes are reviewed, if the escape of our army from Canada was not countenanced by Sir Guy Carleton, it must appear miraculous."[48] What Wilkinson did not know was that Carleton had told Burgoyne to follow the enemy closely, "but without hazarding anything till the column on the right should be able to co-operate."[49] Carleton would never take a chance on a battle without everything in his favour.

With the recovery of the burning ruins of Fort St. Jean, the pursuit was at an end. Lorimier, who had returned to Montreal when Arnold decamped, collected a few Indians and hurried to intercept the retreating American bateaux at a narrow passage in the river between St. Jean and Ile aux Noix. But he arrived too late. The enemy had passed the critical point and had landed on the swampy island from which they had launched their initial operations against St. Jean. However, they did not choose to remain in that malarial atmosphere, and by the beginning of July were back in Crown Point. Thus, within ten months, the two armies which had set out in September 1775 to conquer Canada had been reduced, by what Dr. Senter, who had accompanied them throughout the whole campaign, described as "a heterogeneal concatenation of the most peculiar and unparalleled rebuffs and sufferings that are perhaps to be found in the annals of any nation,"[50] to a humiliated, demoralized wreck whose retreat from Quebec was marked by a long line of graves. "The subject is disgusting to me — I will dismiss it," cried Samuel Adams, in anger and frustration.[51]

IV. The Destruction of Arnold's Fleet on Lake Champlain

But dismiss it Adams could not. Crown Point and Ticonderoga, even though they had been torn from Canada by the boundary settlement of 1763, were still, from a strategic point of view, the military keys to the water highway which led to Canada and to the St. Lawrence. Their recovery by Carleton was therefore a strategic necessity for the defence of Canada against a renewal of the American invasion and for any offensive operations against the rebellious colonies. But before Carleton was prepared to lead his troops towards Crown Point and Ticonderoga he believed it essential to regain naval control of Lake Champlain. He made this quite clear in a letter to Lord George Germain. "The Operations of the Army against the Rebels must now be suspended for some time. Great difficulties occur in transporting provisions, Artillery Stores, &c overland from Chambly, to St. John's and providing the Boats and armed Vessels necessary for Lake Champlain."[52] Good staff officer that he was, Carleton had foreseen this

Philip Skene's sawmill and blockhouse, Fort Anne's Creek, South Bay, where Arnold obtained lumber to build his ships. Later burned by the Americans during Burgoyne's counter-invasion 1777.

problem even while engaged in planning the defence of Quebec. Before his naval adviser, Captain Thomas Pringle, had returned to England in November 1775, Carleton had urged him to make representations to the Admiralty for the early despatch to Canada in 1776 of a number of flat-bottomed boats and other pre-fabricated boat building materials, "ready to be joyned together with all their apparatus for rigging, arming &c."[53] Only ten of the boats had arrived and Carleton had, perforce, to set out to build more at St. Jean. He placed Brigadier General William Phillips in charge of the task of the construction of a fleet of boats which could operate on Lake Champlain and assist in the recovery of the former Canadian forts. With the assistance of several naval officers, including Captain Pringle, Captain Charles Douglas, Lieutenant Dacres and Lieutenant John Schanck, "their Sailors also with the Masters and seamen of the Transports . . . and all the Artificers" available, Phillips made St. Jean into a major ship-building centre during the summer of 1776. And it occupied the entire summer. Even as late as September 28th, Carleton was writing in his customary lugubrious style, this time to Lord George Germain, who had succeeded Lord Dartmouth, "The Rebels have at the entrance of the Lake a considerable naval Force; and I expect our Fleet will soon sail with hopes of success should they come to action: . . . Unfortunately the season is so far advanced that I dare not flatter myself we shall be able to do more this summer than draw off their attention and keep back part of their Force from General Howe,"[54] who had launched a major operation against Long Island opposite the city of New York.

While the carpenters and the sailors were wielding their saws and their hammers at St. Jean, Carleton was free to turn his attention to other pressing problems, military and political. He established his headquarters in Montreal and detached a battalion of regulars to garrison the city. He re-opened communications with Forster in Oswegatchie; authorized the Canadian militiamen to return home and thanked them for their services; established a new supply depot at Chambly and found quarters for the large concentration of troops in the villages along the Richelieu. Carleton also welcomed the arrival of Sir John Johnson and two hundred volunteers from the Mohawk Valley and, "taking it for granted that the King's pleasure is, not only to furnish all his good and Loyal Subjects, with the means of defending themselves against rapine and violence, but further to grant them all possible assistance," gave Johnson a commission to raise a battalion to be known as The King's Royal Regiment of New York.[55] Then, having done all he could to facilitate the preparations for his contemplated operations on Lake Champlain, Carleton hastened to Quebec to undertake the reorganization of the law courts. His attitude towards the Canadians who had supported Congress was one of conciliation, and the penalties which were visited upon the malcontents were largely of an ecclesiastical nature, administered through Bishop Briand, rather than criminal and administered by the courts. However, it was now time to re-open the civilian courts once again, to fill the

Horatio Gates

vacancies on the bench occasioned by the imprisonment by the Americans of two judges from Montreal, and to issue commissions of justice of the peace. Then, his work in Quebec completed, Carleton returned to Montreal on August 17th.

During July and August the only military activity on either side took the form of patrolling. In this way the general officers of both the British and the American forces were able to keep in touch with each other and ascertain what action, if any, was being planned by their opponents. Sometimes the reconnaissance patrols ended in shooting and in the capture of a small number of prisoners, such as that led by Captain James H. Craig of the 47th on July 2nd, which went to Ile La Motte. At other times, patrols penetrated as far as Crown Point, bringing back information about the presence of Americans at that place, such as that led by the Sieur de Boucherville on July 29th. On one occasion an American patrol, led by Benjamin Whitcomb, ambushed and killed Brigadier General Gordon, who was returning on his horse to Laprairie after visiting General Fraser at St. Jean. The manner of Gordon's death led to great indignation on the part of the British. "A Melancholly thing," wrote one British soldier, "that an old Officer, who had served with honour all last War in America, should single and unarmed fall a Victim to a Cowardly Assassin, who dare not shew his

Face in Action, but glories in committing Murder in the Dark."[56] A number of Americans felt likewise about Gordon's death, if we may believe James Wilkinson,[57] although this number did not apparently include Whitcomb's superiors who subsequently promoted him in rank. Frequently patrols were sent out to capture deserters, particularly those Americans who had readily joined Maclean's corps after the failure of American arms before Quebec, and who found it difficult to resist the temptation to desert again, now that they were so near their own land. Most of the patrol actions were carried out by Canadian Indians who, by early September, numbered no fewer than 641, according to a count by General Phillips.[58]

While the British were busy constructing their fleet of boats at St. Jean, the Americans were equally busy reorganizing their forces to meet the threat which they knew would become a reality before the year was out. Their first step was to appoint a new commanding officer, Major General Horatio Gates, who was given command of the northern army and was made "dictator in Canada for six months."[59] Both Sullivan and Schuyler were offended by the appointment but, although a *modus vivendi* was arrived at by Gates and Schuyler whereby Gates commanded at Ticonderoga and Schuyler at Albany, Sullivan simply resigned his appointment and stormed off to Philadelphia to take up the matter with Congress. Arriving at the pest-ridden mess at Lake Champlain, Gates decided that there was no point in trying to hold on to Crown Point and ordered its evacuation, despite Washington's opinion that a decision of this nature should have been left to Congress. The evacuation was completed by the middle of July. Only a token force — and three hundred — remained behind. Congress gave every assistance to Gates. Reinforcements poured into Ticonderoga during the summer months, soldiers from the Continental Army, militia from the New England states, several companies of artillery and one company of Stockbridge Indians. It is difficult to ascertain just how many men were assembled by Gates, although 9000–10000 men would not be an unfair estimate.

In addition to strengthening his army, Gates set out to make his position on Lake Champlain as strong as possible. New works were constructed on Mount Independence, and new breastworks, redoubts and batteries were erected on the lower levels before Ticonderoga itself. At the same time Arnold was hard at work building up the American lake fleet. Skene's sawmills at Skenesborough were taken over and as the lumber slid out of the mills, it was promptly turned into gondolas and gunboats by carpenters imported from Pennsylvania and Connecticut. As soon as the vessels were ready, they sailed to Crown Point as the principal and most convenient assembly point for the fleet.

By October Carleton was ready to move. Although a General Order had been issued from Chambly on September 8th commanding all British regiments to "hold themselves in readiness to embark, in order to go in quest

The American gunboat *Philadelphia*, sunk during the battle of Valcour Island, October 4, 1776. Raised in 1935, the boat is now in the Smithsonian Institution in Washington, U.S.A. It shows the size and armament of the gunboats which played an important role during the battle, both on the British and American sides.

Another view of the gunboat *Philadelphia*.

of the Rebels,"[60] it was not until a month later that the first movement actually began. On October 7th Fraser's corps was instructed to march to Pointe au Fer on the west shore of Lake Champlain, and from there the advanced guard of the British army could see Pringle's fleet as it set sail from Ile La Motte on October 9th to try conclusions with Benedict Arnold. It was a magnificent sight; three schooners, *Inflexible*, *Maria* and *Carleton*, mounting eighteen, fourteen and twelve guns respectively, led off, followed by *Thunderer*, a large "radeau" or gun ketch, carrying two large howitzers, six 24 pounders and six 12 pounders; then came *Loyal Convert*, a gondola captured from the Americans and armed with six 9 pounders, twelve gun boats, each carrying two 24 pounders, and about fifty flat-bottomed

A contemporary water-colour sketch by C. Randle, showing Pringle's squadron approaching Valcour Island. The large vessels included, from left to right, *Carleton*, *Inflexible*, *Maria*, *Loyal Convert* and *Thunderer*. In the background are the British gunboats.

provision boats or bateaux. To withstand this force Arnold had two schooners, including *Royal Savage*, which had been re-floated at St. Jean by the Americans, armed with fourteen guns, and *Revenge* of eight light weight cannon; two cutters, *Lee* and *Enterprise*, of six and ten guns respectively; three row galleys, well armed with ten to sixteen guns including two 24 pounders; and eight gondolas, or "gundalows" as they were called, including *Philadelphia*, each of three guns, one of which was a 12 pounder carried in the bow. The American water craft apparently carried more guns than did the British, but the latter had an advantage in total weight of metal. Moreover, the British gunners were drawn from the regular artillery companies, both British and German, and were experts at handling their weapons. The seamen were provided by the Royal Navy and the civilian transports; a company of the 29th Regiment went aboard each of the larger vessels to act as marines.

Arnold had been scouting the northern waters of Lake Champlain some time before Pringle was ready to leave St. Jean. As early as September 3rd reports reached St. Jean that an American fleet was in the vicinity of Pointe au Fer. Burgoyne's men lay on their arms that night expecting an attack, but when nothing happened the British general sent scouts to ascertain where and in what strength the enemy were to be found. On September 6th one of these patrols, commanded by Lieutenant Scott of the 24th Regiment, fell in with a boat crew of *Enterprise*, killing and wounding several of them. The American vessel responded by cannonading the woods on shore, to no effect except to alarm the American troops at Crown Point and spread the rumour that the bloodybacks were on the way. Arnold cruised around the lake without finding anything to justify the rumour and then finally decided to moor his vessels under the protection of Valcour Island. The water between the island and the mainland was deep enough for the purposes of navigation

A contemporary water-colour sketch by C. Randle, showing Arnold's vessels at Valcour Island. They include, from left to right, *Revenge, Washington, Philadelphia, Congress, Jersey, Lee, Royal Savage* (with flag), *Boston, New Haven, Providence, Connecticut, New York, Enterprise, Trumbull.*

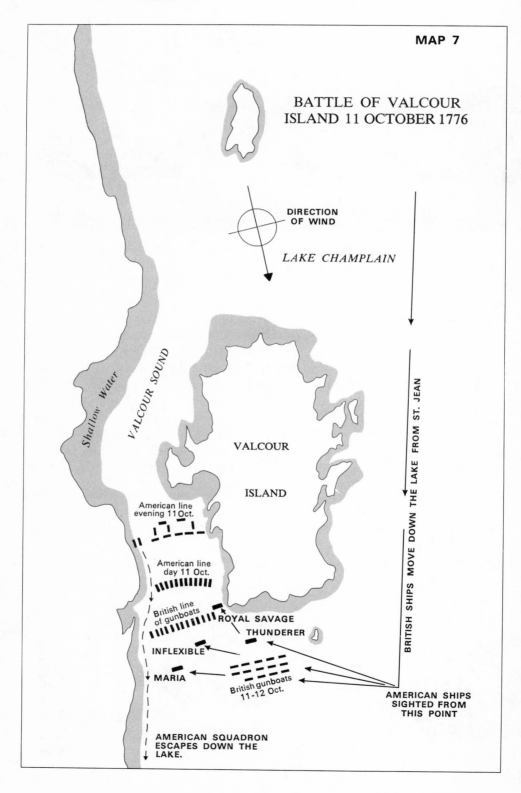

MAP 7

BATTLE OF VALCOUR
ISLAND 11 OCTOBER 1776

DIRECTION
OF WIND

LAKE CHAMPLAIN

Shallow Water

VALCOUR SOUND

VALCOUR

ISLAND

BRITISH SHIPS MOVE DOWN THE LAKE FROM ST. JEAN

American line
evening 11 Oct.

American line
day 11 Oct.

British line
of gunboats

ROYAL SAVAGE

THUNDERER

INFLEXIBLE

MARIA

British gunboats
11-12 Oct.

AMERICAN SHIPS
SIGHTED FROM
THIS POINT

AMERICAN SQUADRON
ESCAPES DOWN THE
LAKE.

Contemporary water colour sketch of the battle of Valcour Island by H. Gilder. It depicts Pringle's squadron engaging Arnold behind an advance screen of gunboats. Carleton's flagship *Maria* is under furled canvas in the foreground. *Loyal Convert* and the radeau *Thunderer* are attempting to move within effective range.

and yet sheltered enough to afford protection from stormy seas and from prying enemy eyes. Here Arnold could await in relative safety the arrival of several new row galleys expected from Skenesborough. If the British ships did find him they would have to beat up wind to get at him, thus giving him the advantage of manoeuvre. Arnold placed his vessels in line across the pass, grouped in three divisions; he himself occupied the centre position with his command headquarters on *Congress*, and General David Waterbury and Colonel Edward Wigglesworth on his right and left respectively. "This disposition," wrote Gates, "will teach the captains of the vessels to know their commanding officers, and prevent any confusion or dispute about command in case an unlucky shot, or other accident, should take off the general."[61]

Guy Carleton did not rush into battle. He paused at Ile La Motte while scouting parties searched the region for signs of Arnold's fleet. Then he moved cautiously up the lake. On the night of October 10-11th he anchored about fifteen miles away from the waters where Arnold was hiding. The next morning, as the British fleet sailed southwards, scudding before a brisk wind, *Inflexible* suddenly sighted an American scouting boat and with several other British vessels, endeavoured to follow it around the south end of Valcour Island. There Carleton and Pringle discovered Arnold's fleet drawn up and ready for battle. Pringle had made the initial error of not having examined the channel west of Valcour Island and now his vessels had to claw their way north into the teeth of the wind. This was difficult for the larger sailing craft such as *Inflexible*, and particularly for the heavy, wallowing *Thunderer*. Arnold had detached *Royal Savage* and *Enterprise* to entice the British into attacking under unfavourable conditions; once the British were committed, they were to hurry back into line. *Carleton*, being nearest the island and to the two American ships, pursued and caught the wind-buffeted *Royal Savage*, which ran aground on the west shore of Valcour Island, with a crashing broadside. Here she was a sitting duck for *Carleton*'s fire. Finally the one-time British vessel was abandoned by her green, inexperienced crew, and left to be burned by a British boarding party. *Carleton* did not come off unscathed. She was engaged by two American row galleys and by American gunboats and suffered extensive damage, her captain, James Dacres, being so badly injured that for the rest of the battle she was fought by a young midshipman, Edward Pellew.

Meanwhile the British gunboats, by using the oars, advanced to within 350 yards of Arnold's line, and it was they who bore the brunt of the battle

A modern pictorial representation of the battle Valcour Island.

from the British side; of the larger craft only *Carleton* ever got into effective cannon range of the Americans. The battle raged for some hours. The gondola *Philadelphia* was sunk, and a British gunboat blew up when an unlucky shot hit her magazine. The operation from the British side was directed by Captain Pringle in *Maria*, on board which vessel stood Carleton himself as an onlooker rather than as a participant. About five o'clock the firing ceased, much to the chagrin of a large contingent of Indians who had accompanied Carleton's fleet in their canoes and who had landed on the island and on the mainland and harrassed the crews of the American vessels with their long range musket fire. The British gunboats had run out of ammunition, and fell back within the protection of the larger British vessels. According to Lieutenant James Hadden of the Royal Artillery, who commanded one of the British gunboats, "little more than 1/3 of the British Fleet"[62] saw much in the way of action at Valcour Island.

Owing to his losses in ships and manpower — sixty killed and wounded and two vessels sunk — Arnold's officers questioned whether there was any point to further resistance. For a naval engagement the casualties were comparatively small but the officers were land based men and losses of ten per cent seemed substantial. In any event, a council of war held on board *Congress* agreed to make an attempt to break through the cordon of gunboats that Pringle had placed across the exit from Valcour Bay. It was certainly worth the effort. It was a dark night; only the embers of *Royal Savage* threw any light upon the water. And in the darkness of October 11-12th the Americans managed to sail their battered and ill-built flotilla through Pringle's blockade. Colonel Wigglesworth's *Trumbull* led the way, hugging the gloom of the western shoreline; the other vessels followed, with Arnold in *Congress* bringing up the rear. There was no sound, as the wind was in their favour. And when Pringle awakened the next morning all he could see was bare water where previously there had been an American fleet. Puzzled as to what course to follow, he did nothing. He dallied for twenty-four hours and then set out in pursuit on the 13th. When finally, a few miles short of Crown Point, he did catch up with Arnold's slowly moving vessels, he concentrated the fire of his heavier ships, *Inflexible*, *Maria* and *Carleton* principally upon *Congress*. Some of the gondolas managed to escape, but *Washington* struck its colours, Waterbury and his men becoming prisoners; *New Jersey* also gave up and *Lee* ran aground to escape further casualties. Hulled again and again by British fire, Arnold finally turned *Congress* towards the shore, where, followed by several other gondolas, he grounded on the shale. After setting fire to his vessels, Arnold made his way through the woods towards Chimney Point, narrowly escaping an Indian ambush on the way. At Chimney Point he found several gondolas including one which had taken no part in the fighting, and going aboard, he and his companions made their way to Crown Point.[63]

Pringle had won a victory, but scarcely a brilliant one. This was the conclusion of some of his junior officers, including Lieutenant John Schanck commanding *Inflexible*, who did not hesitate to criticize his superior officer's inept management of the battle on the first day. Nothing, however, came of the criticisms and Pringle, along with Schanck, Dacres and Pellew, went on to become admirals in the Royal Navy, Pellew being elevated to the peerage as Lord Exmouth.

Crown Point could offer no real refuge to Arnold's men. It had only a small garrison and virtually no works of any value. The Americans therefore burned what they could, including the local sawmill, and continued on their way to Ticonderoga. On the following day the blackened, deserted fortifications of Crown Point were occupied by a group of Indians and soldiers commanded by Captain Craig. Several days later, on the 17th, Fraser's corps took possession of the fort. They were now only twelve miles from Gates at Ticonderoga. At long last Carleton was in a position to launch an offensive against the fort which Ethan Allen had captured from the British by his own peculiar mixture of bluff and courage eighteen months before. Pringle's ships had control of the lake, and Carleton had the means of moving his men and supplies where and when he wished. It was true that the Americans could muster some 9000 men at Ticonderoga, but many of them were militia lacking discipline and stomach for too much hard fighting. Washington, overestimating Carleton's initiative, began to wonder if the British commander might try to by-pass Fort Ticonderoga and march directly upon Albany, but Carleton never really reached the point of giving serious thought to an attack upon Ticonderoga itself, much less pushing into the heart of New York. Such an action would have been out of character. What was in character was his collecting the prisoners taken from Arnold's fleet, giving them a lecture, praising them for their bravery and then releasing them and sending them home on condition that they would agree not to serve again against the British until regularly exchanged. He may have hoped that his continued kindness to the Americans would have a dissolving effect upon the determination of the people of the colonies to continue their resistance. This was how Gates regarded it and why he was at pains to ensure that Carleton's former prisoners did not dally about Fort Ticonderoga weakening the resolve of his militiamen to fight by their dangerous talk.

For another two weeks Carleton's troops hung around the environs of Ticonderoga. On October 27th Fraser pushed to within three miles of the American position, perhaps with the object of enticing Gates to come out from behind his walls, but Gates was no more disposed to move out of Ticonderoga than Carleton had been to move out of Quebec. "Not a Man of the Cowardly Crew dare show himself out of his Strong hold," was how one British officer put it.[64] At first Carleton planned to refurbish the barracks at Crown Point, but changing his mind, he ordered the stores to be sent back to St. Jean, and early in November the British troops returned to Canada. It was not universally a popular move. One, at least, of Carleton's officers regarded it with disgust when he wrote, "this little Army, I say, after having done as much as the Situation of the Country, and the Climate wo'd admit of, by driving the Enemy from Canada, destroying their Fleet, and then following close to their Dens, was obliged to return to Canada to its great Regret, which it did the 2nd November in a very regular manner, without being in the least molested by the enemy, and the Whole got into their Winter Cantonnment abt. the 12th of the same Month."[65]

While the troops were going into winter quarters at various points along the Richelieu from Ile aux Noix to Sorel, and along the St. Lawrence from Longueuil to Kamouraska, Carleton went back to Quebec. Here, on December 31st, Bishop Briand celebrated mass in the Basilica, and those Canadians who had showed too openly their sympathies with the rebels, did public penance at that time. In the evening the governor gave a dinner for sixty guests, followed by a public fete and a grand ball. It was exactly twelve months since they had hurled back the American invasion army led by Montgomery and Arnold.

V Rumours of War 1777-1779

I. The Marquis de LaFayette and Plans for another Invasion

The invaders were gone. Would they come back again? There seemed to be no danger in 1777 of such a possibility. There were now 10,000 troops in Canada, and taking 7000 of them with him, General John Burgoyne planned to carry out a counter-invasion of the colonies, henceforth to be called The United States of America. But Burgoyne surrendered at Saratoga on October 17th and the frontier of Canada, stripped of most of its troops, was open in the autumn of 1777, inviting a repeat of the invasion of 1775. Carleton had, therefore, to turn his attention once more to the defence of Canada. He knew that he did not have the men to hold the forts on Lake Champlain, and promptly issued instructions to Maclean, who commanded at Montreal, to withdraw all troops from Ticonderoga, which had been captured by Burgoyne in July, to St. Jean. But first, Maclean was to destroy the fortifications and burn every building which could possibly be used by an invading American force, on both sides of Lake Champlain all the way to Ile aux Noix. Scorched earth might deter even if it would not halt an enemy attack. At the same time Carleton ordered all his available troops to move into the villages along the Richelieu River from Sorel to St. Jean, in order to minimize any delay which might be encountered in concentrating them to meet the invader. To strengthen the regulars, he persuaded his council to adopt a militia ordinance which would require all male inhabitants between 16 and 60 years of age to be enrolled in the militia and to be regularly instructed in musketry. Officers and men would be drafted from the various militia companies as they might be required. To show his gratitude for their services in 1776 and to hold their support in 1777 Carleton announced the issue of gratuities to all militiamen who had seen service during the campaigns of 1776 and 1777.[1]

There was some justification for these measures. Excited by the surrender of Burgoyne and by the arrival of the nineteen year old romantic, Marie Joseph Paul Roch Yves Gilbert Motier, Marquis de LaFayette, the

145

Le Marquis de Lafayette.
By C. W. Peale, 1781.

more bellicose members of Congress began to think again of invading Canada and adopted a resolution early in January 1778 in favour of another military expedition against Canada, this time under the command of LaFayette. But Congress had not thought fit to consult their own commander in chief, George Washington, and Washington regarded the project with a cold eye. He had enough to do elsewhere, trying to beat the British and ensure the preservation of the revolution and the independence of the new United States. He saw little advantage in becoming embroiled in what he regarded as a dubious political side-show in Canada. Moreover he had serious doubts about the military ability of LaFayette, even if the latter's national origin might attract some Canadians to his colours, and even if he was to be seconded by such experienced officers as the Baron de Kalb, Thomas Conway and John Stark.

LaFayette, despite his early enthusiasm for a project which he hoped might end in the recovery of Canada by France, soon began to have doubts about it too. When he arrived at Albany he did not find the army he had been led to expect; instead of the 2500 men he had been assured would be ready, he was greeted by only 960 miserable looking individuals, a number of them "boys of twelve or patriarchs of sixty ... quite unfit for the proposed march,"[2] and lacking arms and clothing. Schuyler and Arnold, both of whom had vivid recollections of the 1775-1776 attempt to conquer

Canada, were opposed to what they felt was nothing more than a half-baked scheme concocted by Gates for his own self-glorification, and pressed by Gates's supporters in Congress. Moses Hazen and a few expatriate Canadians were enthusiastic, because it was the only way to recover their lost property in Canada. LaFayette never wholly abandoned the idea of the Canada expedition; but Washington did not want to see French power restored on the St. Lawrence, and when the members of Congress began to think about it, neither did they. Canada as a French colony would encourage Americans to look again to Great Britain for assistance, and this would imperil the revolution. Thus, on January 1st, 1779, Congress voted to defer indefinitely the invasion of the north.[3]

Meanwhile the Canadian authorities did not relax their vigilance. Carleton's successor as governor of Canada, Sir Frederick Haldimand, continued his predecessor's precautions, reviving the law authorizing the arrest of those guilty or suspected of treason, keeping a close watch over foreign agents and foreign propaganda, and maintaining constant frontier patrols. And in so doing he relied upon the continued support of those French Canadians who had been loyal to Carleton, men like Neveu-Sevestre and Dupré in Montreal, Tonnancour in Trois Rivières and Baby in Quebec.[4] He even took steps to establish a naval force on Lake Ontario under the command of Jean Baptiste Bouchette to prevent a flank move of the kind used by Amherst in 1760. British posts were maintained at Pointe au Fer and at Ile aux Noix. An additional redoubt was built at St. Jean, now guarded by a hundred or more cannon and a large garrison. There was also a strong force of regulars in Montreal; Sir John Johnson's King's Royal Regiment of New York was at Laprairie, and those Brunswickers who had not been with Burgoyne covered the road between Montreal and the Richelieu. If the Americans came they would meet stiff opposition.

But the Americans never came again. Not, at least, during the Revolutionary War. Thirty-six years were to elapse before another American Congress made a second attempt to finish the work Montgomery and Arnold had failed to complete in 1775-1776.

II. Epilogue, or What Happened to the Dramatis Personae

The Americans who participated in the events of 1775-1776 in Canada played out their roles in history in a variety of fashions. *Samuel Adams* signed the Declaration of Independence in 1776, became lieutenant governor 1789-1794 and governor until 1797 of Massachusetts. He died in 1803. *Ethan Allen*, who captured Ticonderoga, was sent to Great Britain and later to New York where he remained a British prisoner until he was exchanged in May 1778. In 1780 he took part in the negotiations to bring Vermont under the British flag. He died in 1789. *Benedict Arnold*, who took a notable part in the campaign of 1777, entered into correspondence with the British in

John Joseph Henry, a member of Arnold's overland expedition in 1775.

1780 and became a British brigadier general. After living briefly in St. John and Fredericton, he went to England where he remained until his death in 1801. Two of his sons settled in Upper Canada. *John Brown* continued in the American army and was killed in an ambuscade at Stone Arabia on the Mohawk River in 1780. *Isaac Butterfield* and *Timothy Bedel* were both placed under arrest and sent to Sorel, but owing to the retreat of the army, were not court-martialed until August 1776 in Fort Ticonderoga. Both were sentenced to be cashiered and incapacitated from ever again holding an American commission. *Bedel* was subsequently reinstated and was directed to investigate the feasibility of an invasion route into Canada via the St. Francis River. He became a major general of the New Hampshire militia and died in 1787. *Horatio Gates*, following his victory over Burgoyne at Saratoga in 1777, hoped to displace Washington as commander in chief, but following his defeat at Camden in 1780 he was court-martialed and superseded. He retired to Virginia and then to New York where he died in 1806. *John Joseph Henry* studied law, was admitted to the bar and became judge of the 2nd District of Pennsylvania. He died in 1811 at the age of fifty-two. *The Marquis de LaFayette* continued to serve under Washington during the Revolutionary War and was present at the surrender of Cornwallis at Yorktown. In France he played a prominent part in the early years of the French Revolution. Distrusted both by the Jacobins and the Court he fled to

Liège and was imprisoned by the Austrians. Liberated by Napoleon in 1797 he refrained from political activity until the restoration of the Bourbons when he again took the side of the opposition. He played a role in the Revolution of 1830 and commanded the National Guard. He died in 1834 without having won the affection of any party in France, although revered by the Americans as a hero. In 1824 he was given a large purse of money and a township of land in the United States. *Philip Schuyler* resigned his command in 1779, but continued to serve the United States as Indian Commissioner. He remained active in political life until 1797 and died in Albany in 1804. *Dr. Isaac Senter* retired from the American army in 1779 and practised medicine, first in Cranston, Rhode Island, and later in Newport. He died in 1799 at the age of forty-six. *John Sullivan* resigned his commission after the appointment of Gates in 1776. Withdrawing his resignation at the request of Congress, he joined Washington, fought at Brandywine, and Germantown and Butts' Hill. In 1779 he led the campaign against the Iroquois but failed to oust Butler from Niagara. After the war he entered politics, became a judge and died in 1795. *David Wooster* resigned his commission after the American retreat from Canada, but accepted a major general's commission in the Connecticut State Militia. He was surprised by Governor Tryon's raid on Ridgefield and was fatally wounded in the battle in April 1777.

Of the English merchants who turned traitor and helped the Americans, only one returned to Canada. After leaving Quebec, *Edward Antill* joined Montgomery as his chief engineer. Subsequently he was appointed lieutenant colonel of Hazen's regiment of Canadians. Captured by the British at Staten Island in 1777, he remained a prisoner until exchanged in 1780. He lived in New York until 1785 when he returned to Canada and died in St. Jean in 1789. *Moses Hazen* commanded in Montreal between Wooster and Arnold. In 1777 he was court-martialed in Fort Ticonderoga as a result of a quarrel with Arnold but was exonerated. He was appointed quarter master general of the force LaFayette proposed to lead into Canada. In 1781 he became a brigadier general. After the Revolutionary War he settled in Vermont and died in 1802. *James Livingston* was the first to recruit Canadians on behalf of Congress. He continued to serve in the American army during the remainder of the Revolutionary War. He was present at Stillwater and at Saratoga in 1777. He remained in the United States and died in Saratoga county, New York, in 1832. *James Price* and *Thomas Walker* fled from Canada with Arnold's troops in 1777 and disappeared into well-deserved obscurity after Mrs. Walker's bitter tongue had accused the three commissioners from Congress of being pro-British and betraying the trust Congress had placed in them. Apparently Walker went to England, for Pierre du Calvet met him in London in 1785.

Thomas Ainslie carried the temporary rank of captain in the British militia and served throughout the siege of Quebec. He remained collector of customs, the office to which he had been appointed in 1762, until 1799. It is not certain when he died. He was apparently still alive in 1818. *Guy Carleton*, knighted for his services during the American invasion, nevertheless retired from his appointment in Canada in 1778 as a result of differences between himself and Lord George Germain. In 1782 he accepted the appointment of commander in chief in North America and went to New York where he superintended the evacuation of the Loyalists at the end of the Revolutionary War. In 1786 he returned to Canada as governor for a second time with the title of Baron Dorchester. Ten years later he retired to England and died in 1808. *Hector Cramahé* retained his appointment as lieutenant governor until 1782. In 1785 he was appointed lieutenant governor of Detroit, but did not take up his duties there. He died in England in 1788. *John Burgoyne* led the counter-invasion of the United States in 1777 which came to a disastrous conclusion at Saratoga on October 16th. He was, in consequence, deprived of his appointments. He returned to England where he demanded a court-martial but did not get it. Although his appointments were restored to him in 1782, he retired to private life and occupied his time writing plays. He died in 1792. *Simon Fraser*, lieutenant colonel of the 24th Regiment, became brigadier general June 9th, 1776. He played a notable part in the campaign of 1777 in the capture of Ticonderoga and in the battles of Hubbardton and Freeman's Farm. He died of wounds sustained at Bemis Heights, October 8th, 1777. *Guy Johnson* succeeded his uncle, Sir William, as superintendent of Indian affairs for New York in 1774. He moved to Canada in 1775 and with Joseph Brant went to England prior to the fall of Montreal. In 1776 he returned to New York and in 1778 took part in the raids on the Mohawk Valley. He subsequently returned to England and died in London in 1788. *Sir John Johnson*, the son of Sir William, remained on his father's estate until 1776 when he was compelled to flee to Canada with a large number of his tenants, because of his royal sympathies. In 1776 he organized and commanded The King's Royal Regiment of New York which took part in a number of frontier engagements during the Revolutionary War. In 1783 he became superintendent general of Indian affairs. He was the choice of the Loyalists for the first lieutenant governor of Upper Canada, but the appointment went to John Graves Simcoe. He became a member of the Legislative council of Lower Canada in 1796 and held this appointment until his death in 1830. *Allan Maclean*, who played so important a role during the siege of Quebec, was promoted brigadier general on June 6th, 1777 and was placed in command in Montreal, where he remained until peace was signed in 1783. He retired from active service, having raised two regiments, the 114th Royal Highland Volunteers (1761) and the 84th Royal Highland Emigrants (1775). He died in 1797. *William Nesbitt*, lieutenant colonel of the 47th, was promoted brigadier general June 9th, 1776. He took sick during the campaign and returned to

François Baby fought on the Canadian side during the Seven Years' War but after two years in France returned to Canada and became a staunch supporter of British rule. In 1774 he was appointed a member of the Council and took a prominent part against the Americans.

Quebec where he died shortly after the British withdrawal from Crown Point. *Edward Pellew* distinguished himself as a ship commander during the Wars of the French Revolution. He was knighted in 1793, was elected to Parliament, became a rear admiral in 1804 and commander in chief of the East India Station. In 1811 he became commander in chief in the Mediterranean and in 1814 became admiral of the blue, and was elevated to the peerage as Baron Exmouth. He died in 1833. *Richard Prescott* taken prisoner in 1775 was exchanged in 1776. He became third in command of the British Army in North America until he was made prisoner a second time in 1777. Released the same year he became a major general. In 1782 he became a lieutenant general. He died in 1788.

Most of those Canadians who had remained loyal throughout the period of the invasion were subsequently rewarded for their loyalty with government appointments. *François Baby* took a prominent part in the defence of Canada during the invasion. He was a captain of one of the Canadian militia companies in Quebec, and in 1777 was appointed to the Council of the province of Quebec. In 1781 he became Adjutant General of militia. In 1791 he became a member of the executive council of Lower Canada and a leading member of the so-called "Chateau Clique." He died in Montreal in 1820. *Louis Liénard de Beaujeu* took part in the siege of St. Jean. Released after the surrender of the fort he retired from the service to his manoir on the Ile aux Grues. He organized a militia force to assist Carleton in March 1776, the

Mgr. Jean Olivier Briand, Bishop of Quebec, who supported Carleton and instructed the Roman Catholic clergy that religion, honour and interest required them to obey the government's orders.

advance guard of which was betrayed and defeated at the engagement at St. Pierre du Sud. He died in 1802. *François Marie Picoté de Belestre* took the oath of allegiance after the fall of Detroit in 1760. He was taken prisoner by the Americans at St. Jean and died in 1793. *Jean Baptiste Bouchette* had served during the Seven Years' War and then gone into the fishing business in the Gulf of St. Lawrence. After helping Carleton to escape from Montreal, he served as commandant of the British naval forces on Lake Ontario. He died at Fort Frederick, Kingston, in 1804. *Bishop Jean Olivier Briand* played an important role in countering the American propaganda during the invasion. He retired on a pension in 1784 and died in 1794. *François Dambourgès* was awarded a commission in The Royal Highland Emigrants for his services as a volunteer during the siege of Quebec. In 1785 he received a commission in the Royal Canadian Volunteers and subsequently became a colonel in the militia. Between 1792 and 1796 he was a member of the Legislative Assembly of Lower Canada. He died in Montreal in 1798. *Malcolm Fraser*, who served at Quebec with The Royal Highland Emigrants, spent the remainder of his life on his seigneury at Malbaie where he died in 1815. *Charles Louis Tarieu de La Naudière* had gone to France after the Seven Years' War and then returned to Canada. After serving as Carleton's aide de camp during the Revolutionary War, he was appointed to the

Gabriel-Elzéar Taschereau, one of Guy Carleton's French Canadian supporters during the American invasion, who took part in the defence of Quebec in 1775. In 1777 he became a judge of the Court of Common Pleas in the District of Montreal.

Legislative Council of Lower Canada in which he sat until his death in 1811. *François Thomas de Verneuil de Lorimier* returned to Canada from France after the Seven Years' War and entered the Canadian Indian service. He led the Indians against Montgomery and was wounded at St. Jean. He took part in the fighting at the Cedars. His brother was killed at the battle of Crysler's Farm in 1813. *Jean Baptiste Pierre Louvigny, Sieur de Montigny*, returned to Canada from France in 1770. He joined Belestre at St. Jean and escaped through the American lines to carry despatches to Carleton. Escaping from Montreal before its surrender, he raised a party of Canadians to take part in the fighting at the Cedars. After the Revolutionary War he entered the fur trade and in 1789 was sent to Detroit by Dorchester. He was commissioned in the Royal Canadian Volunteers, raising a company in the region of Detroit. He was taken prisoner by the Americans during the War of 1812 and was exchanged, but died in 1813. *John Nairne*, a former member of Fraser's Highlanders who served with Maclean's Royal Highland Emigrants at Quebec, retired after the American War to live quietly on his seigneury at Murray Bay, where he died in 1802. *Pierre Méru Panet* was one of the Montreal citizens chosen to negotiate the surrender of Montreal to Montgomery. In 1778 he became a judge of the Court of Common Pleas. He was appointed to the Legislative Council of Lower Canada in 1791 and died in 1804. *Simon Sanguinet* was a notary and lawyer in Montreal and practised both of these professions until 1786. In 1788 he was appointed a judge of the Court of Common Pleas for Montreal. He died two years later. He was the author of *Le Témoin Oculaire*. *Gabriel Elzéar Taschereau* took part in the defence of Quebec and in the fighting at the Sault au Matelot. In 1776 he was appointed a member of the commission to determine the extent of damages suffered by the people of Montreal during the invasion, and in 1777 became a judge. Because of his interests in Quebec and La Beauce, he resigned and returned to Quebec. He sat as a member of the Legislative Assembly of Lower Canada between 1792 and 1796 and in 1798 was appointed to the Legislative Council. He died in 1809. *Marie Joseph Godefroy de Tonnancour* was educated in Quebec, Paris and Oxford. He was taken prisoner by the Americans in 1775 and was exchanged in 1777. In 1792 he was elected to the legislature of Lower Canada but withdrew from politics in 1793 to devote his time to his seigneury. In 1812 he again took up arms against the Americans. He died in 1834.

> 'Tis not the least disparagement
> To be defeated by th' event,
> Nor to be beaten by main force,
> That does not make a man the worse;
> But to turn tail, and run away,
> And without blows give up the day,
> Or to surrender ere th' assault
> That's no man's fortune, but his fault.
>
> (Samuel Butler, *Hubridas*)

Appendices

Appendix I
The Officers of the 1st Battalion of The Royal Highland Emigrants 1779

Rank	Name	Rank in the Regiment	Army
Colonel	Sir H. Clinton, K.B.	16 Dec 1778	Lt. Gen. 29 Aug 77
Lt. Col. Command	Allan Maclean	12 June 1775	25 May 72
Major	Donald McDonald	12 June 1775	Lt. Col. 29 Aug 77
Captain	William Dunbar	13 June 1775	
	John Nairne	14 do.	Major 29 Aug 77
	Colin Campbell	do.	25 May 72
	Alex. Fraser	do.	
	Malcolm Fraser	do.	
	John McDougall	do.	
	Daniel Robertson	do.	
	David Alex. Grant	do.	
Lieutenant	Neil Maclean	14 June 1775	
	John Maclean	do.	
	Lauchlan Maclean	do.	
	Alex. Stratton	do.	
	Arch. Maclean	do.	
	Hector Maclean	do.	
	Fran. Dambourgès	27 Feb 76	
	Donald McKinnon	16 July	
	David Cairns	do.	
	Ranald McDonald	25 Dec.	
	Ranald McDonell	do.	
Ensign	Archibald Grant	12 June 1775	
	John Smith	do.	
	George Dame	do.	
	Hector Maclean	do.	
	Archibald McDonell	27 Feb 76	
	James Pringle	16 July	
	Alex. Fletcher	do.	
	Duncan McDougall	25 Dec	
Chaplain	John Bethune	14 June 1775	
Adjutant	Ranald McDonald	25 do.	
Quarter Master	Lauchlan Maclean	14 do.	
Surgeon	Alex. Davidson	do.	

Appendix II
The Officers of the 1st Battalion of The King's Royal Regiment of New York

Rank	Name	Birthplace	Length of Service (in yrs.)	Former Situation & Remarks
Lt. Colonel, Commandant	Sir John Johnson, Bt.	America	8	Succeeded his father, the late Sir William Johnson, as Major General of the Militia of the Northern District of the Province of New York. Was in possession of nearly 200,000 acres of valuable land lost in consequence of the rebellion.
Major	James Gray	Scotland	26	Ensign in Lord Loudon's Regiment in 1745. Lieutenant & Captain in the 42nd, till after taking the Havannah at which time he sold out. Had some landed property part of which is secured to his son, the remainder lost in conconsequence of the rebellion.
Captains	Angus McDonell	Scotland	25	Ensign in 60th Regiment 8 July 1760. Lieutenant in D^O 27 Dec 1770. Sold out on account of bad state of health 22 May 1775. Had no lands.
	John Munro	Scotland	8	Had considerable landed property lost in consequence of the rebellion, and served last War in America.
	Patrick Daly	Ireland	9	Lieutenant in the 84th regiment at the siege of Quebec 1775 & 6.
	Richard Duncan	Scotland	13	5 years Ensign in the 55th regiment.
	Samuel Anderson	America	8	Had landed property and served last War in America.
	John McDonell	Scotland	8	Had landed property 500 acres purchased and begun to improve in April 1774.
	Alexander McDonell	Scotland	8	200 acres land in fee simple under Sir John Johnson Bt. at the annual rent of £6 per 100.
	Archibald McDonell	Scotland	8	Merchant, had no lands.
Captain Lieutenant	Allan McDonell	Scotland	8	Held 200 acres of land in fee simple under Sir John Johnson at £6 per 100.

Rank	Name	Birthplace	Length of Service (in yrs.)	Former Situation & Remarks
Lieutenants	Malcolm McMartin	Scotland	8	Held 100 acres of land in fee simple under Sir John Johnson at £6 per 100.
	Peter Everitt	America	7	Had some landed property.
	John Prentiss	America	7	A volunteer at the siege of Quebec 1775 & 6.
	Hugh McDonell	Scotland	9	Son of Captain McDonell
	John F. Holland	America	5	Son of Major Holland, Surveyor-General Province Quebec
	William Coffin	America	2	Son of Mr. Coffin, Merchant, late of Boston.
	Jacob Farrand	America	7	Nephew to Major Gray.
	William Claus	America	7	Son of Colonel Claus, Deputy Agent Indian Affairs.
	Hugh Munro	America	6	Son of Captain John Munro
	Joseph Anderson	America	6	Son of Captain Samuel Anderson
	Thomas Smith	Ireland	4	Son of Doctor Smith
Ensigns	John Conelly	Ireland	2	Private Gentleman
	Jacob Glen	America	2	Son of John Glen, Esq. of Schenectady. Had considerable landed property.
	Miles McDonell	Scotland	3	Son of Captain John McDonell
	Ebenezer Anderson	America	6	Son of Captain Samuel Anderson
	Duncan Cameron	Scotland	14	In the service last War preceding this one.
	John Mann	America	6	Private Gentleman.
	Francis McCanty	Ireland	28	Formerly Serjeant in the 34th reigment.
	John Valintine	America	24	18 yrs. in 55th and 62nd Regiments.
Chaplain	John Doty	America	8	Formerly Minister of the Gospel at Schenectady.
Adjutant	James Valintine	Ireland	4	Son of Ensign John Valintine
2nd Master	Isaac Mann	America	8	Merchant
Surgeon	Charles Austin	England	22	14 years as Hospital Mate
Mate	James Steuart	Scotland	14	Surgeon's Mate in the 42nd Regt. the war before last.

Appendix III
The Officers of the Canadian Militia who were Employed during the Siege of Quebec in 1775

	Colonel	Noel Voyer
	Lieutenant Colonel	Lecompte Dupré
	Major	François Baby
	Captaine	Gabriel Elz. Taschereau
	Chirugien	Mr. Badelard
	Secd. Aide Major	Mr. Louis Germain, fils
	Aide Major d'Artillerie	Mr. Guichaud
	Sous Aide Major	Mr. Pierre Perras, fils

Première Compagnie	Capitaine	Jacques Perras
	Capitaine en second	Pierre Dufau
	Lieutenant	Jacques Perrault
	Enseigne	Jean Bte. Panet
	Enseigne	René Marchand
	Premier Sergent	Thomas Morin
	Second Sergent	Joseph Damien

Compagnie des Volontaires	Capitaine	Pierre Marcoux
	Capitaine en second	Joseph Chabot
	Lieutenant	Mr. Bouchaud
	Enseigne	Louis Marchand
	Sergent	Joseph Bonneville

Troisième Compagnie	Capitaine	Charles Berthelot
	Capitaine en second	Louis Corbin
	Lieutenant	Antoine Serindac
	Enseigne	Noel Dupont
	Enseigne	Joseph Noel
	Premier Sergent	François Mignau
	Second Sergent	Antoine Jacson

Quatrième Compagnie	Capitaine	Alexandre Dumas
	Capitaine en second	Louis Fornel
	Lieutenant	Joseph Duval
	Enseigne	Armand Primont
	Premier Sergent	Augustin Lavau
	Second Sergent	Pierre Prate

Cinquième Compagnie	Capitaine	Louis Frémont
	Capitaine en second	Charles Liard
	Lieutenant	Louis Turgeon
	Enseigne	Jean Bte. Chevalier
	Premier Sergent	Jean Chevalier
	Second Sergent	Baptiste Chevalier

Sixième Compagnie	Capitaine	Henry Morin
	Premier Lieutenant	Alexandre Picard
	Lieutenant	Liberal Dumas
	Enseigne	Cureux St. Germain
	Premier Sergent	Canac Marquis
	Second Sergent	Charles Lamontagne
Septième Compagnie	Capitaine	Mr. Launière
	Capitaine en second	Paul Lacroix
	Lieutenant	Pinguet Vaucour
	Enseigne	Jean Bte. Volant
	Enseigne	François Valin
	Premier Sergent	Jean Bte. Durouvray
	Second Sergent	Joseph Lucas
Compagnie d'Artillerie	Capitaine	Henry Laforce
	Capitaine en second	Mr. Pommerau
	Lieutenant	Mr. Lafontaine
	Lieutenant	Mr. Bouchet
	Enseigne	Mr. Bruneau
	Premier Sergent	Alexis Beranger
	Second Sergent	Joseph Quimbert
	Troisième Sergent	Jacques Pampalon
Compagnie pour la Garde des Prisoniers	Capitaine	Mr. Jean François Cugnet
	Capitaine en second	Mr. Pierre Marchant
	Lieutenant	Mr. Boissau
	Enseigne	Louis Robin
	Sergent	François Ray dit Crespin
	Sergent	Devis
	Sergent	Pasquet
	Sergent	François Paul Larivière dit Lavictoire

Recapitulation by Gabriel Taschereau 6 May 1776	Officers	44
	Volontaires et Compagnie des Ecoliers ·	43
	Sergents majors	2
	Sergents	26
	Caporaux	29
	Soldats Miliciens	489
	Tambours	2
	Compagnie pour la garde des prisoniers	74
	Total	710

Appendix IV
The Officers of the British Militia at Quebec as of April 1778

Colonel Commandant	Henry Caldwell
Adjutant	Peter Mills
Quartermaster	James Sinclair
Captains	James Johnson (Artillery)
	Alex. Johnson
	Thomas Ainslie
	Charles Grant
	Edward Harrison
	Robert Lister
Lieutenants	George Gregory (Artillery)
	Richard Murray
	Thomas Scott
	Hugh Finlay
	William Lindsay
Ensigns	John Lee
	Samuel Phillips
	John Renaud
	Meredith Wills

Bibliographical Note

This book is based largely upon materials, Canadian and American, contemporary with the events described therein. The principal manuscript sources are to be found in the Q and B series in the public Archives of Canada. However, for the historian who finds it difficult or impossible to make the long trek to that Mecca of Canadian history students, the Public Archives of Canada in Ottawa, a number of the pertinent documents are available in printed form in A. Shortt and A. G. Doughty (editors), *Documents Relating to the Constitutional History of Canada 1759-1791*, published by the federal Archives, in the second volume of *A History of the Organization, Development and Services of the Military and Naval Forces of Canada from the Peace of Paris in 1763 to the Present Time*, edited by Brigadier-General Ernest Cruikshank, Director of the Historical Section of the Canadian General Staff, in the *Mandements, lettres pastorales et circulaires des Evêques de Québec*, Volume II, edited by Mgr. F. Têtu and Abbé C. O. Gagnon, and published in 1882, and in several volumes of the *Reports of the Canadian Archives*, notably that for 1914 which contains Major Charles Preston's journal and various letters relating to the surrender of St. Jean. The report written by François Baby, Gabriel Taschereau and Jenkin Williams, essential to any understanding of the attitude of the Canadians during the invasion, appears in the *Rapport de l'Archiviste de la Province de Québec* 1927-28. The *Quebec Gazette* for 1775-1776 is, of course, a source as necessary as it is obvious to the historian. The relevant American documentary materials are to be found in several series, IV and V in particular, of *American Archives: consisting of a collection of authentic records, state papers, debates and letters and other notices of public affairs, the whole forming a documentary history of the origin and progress of the North American Colonies etc.*, edited by Peter Force. This collection is most useful to the student, despite the fact that some of the documents are inaccurately transcribed. Rather less useful is the more familiar *Documentary History of the State of New York*, edited by E. B. O'Callaghan.

Fortunately for the historian, a few — one could wish there were more — soldiers were sufficiently of a historical turn of mind and sufficiently literate to keep journals or to write their recollections for the instruction or entertainment of posterity. The Abbé Hospice-Anthelme Verreau collected several of these and published them in his *Invasion du Canada, Collection de Mémoires receuillis et annotés*, published in Montreal in 1873. Among the journals and papers thus preserved were those of Sanguinet, Badeaux, Berthelot and de Lorimier, together with a collection of letters written to and by François Baby. Dealing specifically with the siege of Quebec are the journals of Thomas Ainslie, recently edited and re-published under the title of *Canada Preserved*, by Sheldon S. Cohen, and those published by the Literary and Historical Society of Quebec, under the title of *Blockade of Quebec in 1775-1776 by the American Revolutionists* in 1905. This collection contains several journals and the British Militia Orderly Book at Quebec covering the period between 17 Sept. 1775 and Jun. 1776. For the relief of Quebec and the liberation of Canada in 1776, reference should be had to J. M. Hadden's *Journal Kept in Canada and Upon Burgoyne's Expedition in 1776 and 1777*, Albany, 1887, J. P. Baxter (editor), *The Journal of Lieutenant William Digby, A Journal of the Campaigns against the Americans in 1776 and 1777 conducted from Canada by an officer who served with Lieut. General Burgoyne*, edited by G. F. G. Stanley under the title *For Want of a Horse*, and Friedrich Adolph Riedesel's *Memoirs and Letters of Major General Riedesel, during his residence in America*, Albany, 1868. For a contemporary account of the American defeat at the Cedars and the terms of the surrender, *Authentic Narrative of Facts Relating to the Exchange of Prisoners at the Cedars*, London, 1777, provides the necessary factual information.

Kenneth Roberts, the American historical novelist, placed historians in his debt by collecting a number of the journals of the men who accompanied Arnold in 1775 and publishing them in his *March to Quebec, Journals of the Members of Arnold's Expedition*, New York, 1938. Among them are the accounts written by Arnold himself, as well as those written by Henry Dearborn, Simeon Thayer, Isaac Senter, John Henry and Abner Stocking, and a collection of Arnold's letters. Other useful personal statements by American participants include *The Narrative of Colonel Ethan Allen*, republished in 1961 with an introduction by Brooke Hindle, *A Narrative of the Military Actions of Colonel Marinus Willett*, New York, 1831, and Brantz Mayer's edited version of the *Journal of Charles Carroll of Carrolltown, during his visit to Canada in 1776*, Baltimore, 1876. The *Trumbull Papers* will be found in the collected papers printed by the Massachusetts Historical Society, 1885-1888. James Wilkinson's *Memoirs of My Own Times*, Philadelphia, 1876, has some value for the later part of the Canadian story.

Few Canadians have elected to write specifically on the American invasion of Canada in 1775-1776. In most accounts the story appears as simply an episode in the larger story of Canada and the American Revolution. This, I feel, is to be deplored, if only because the subject is an exciting one and Canadians have every reason to be satisfied with the outcome. Among the most significant Canadian accounts are Gustave Lanctot's *Le Canada et la révolution Américaine*, Montréal, 1965, and Marcel Trudel's *Louis XVI, Le Congrès Américain et le Canada, 1774-1789*, Québec, 1949. A shorter account appears in Claude-Marie Boissonnault's *Histoire politico-militaire des Canadiens-français 1763-1945*, Trois Rivières, 1967. Accounts in English from the Canadian point of view include those in William Kingsford's *History of Canada*, Volumes V and VI, Toronto, 1892, 1893, George M. Wrong's *Canada and the American Revolution*, New York, 1935, and A. L. Burt's *The Old Province of Quebec*, Toronto, 1933.

Americans have been more ready than Canadians to write about their military achievements, even when these achievements have been less than successful. The most detailed treatment of the present subject is to be found in Justin H. Smith's two volumes, entitled *Our Struggle for the Fourteenth Colony*, New York, 1907. Other accounts, such as John Codman's *Expedition to Quebec*, New York, 1902, C. H. Jones's *History of the Campaign for the Conquest of Canada*, Philadelphia, 1882, and B. J. Lossing's *Pictorial Field Book of the Revolution*, New York, 1850-1852, are not to be ignored simply because they are not up to date. Two recent, popular accounts, dealing with the events of 1775 and 1776, have been written by Harrison Bird, *Navies in the Mountains*, New York, 1962, and *Attack on Quebec, The American Invasion of Canada 1775-1776*, New York, 1968. They are short and readable. A more thorough but rather specialized account which has not appeared in print, but ought to, is P. E. Leroy's doctoral thesis, "Sir Guy Carleton as a Military Leader During the American Invasion and Repulse in Canada 1775-1776," Ann Arbour, 1960.

Like the story I have told in the text of this book, this bibliography is neither complete nor exhaustive. The door is still open for any ambitious scholar who would like to fill out what are little more than introductory sketches.

Footnotes

I. The Propaganda War 1774-1775

1. On 15 Feb. 1767, Carleton wrote to General Gage urging the construction of a citadel at Quebec and the repairing of the fortifications of Crown Point, Ticonderoga and Fort George. He also urged upon the British authorities the advisability of raising a Canadian regiment. This letter has sometimes been used as an argument that Carleton was thinking in terms of keeping the American colonies in subjection. Carleton's correspondence, however, makes it clear that Carleton was not thinking as much of the possibility of hostilities with the American colonies as with France. War with France might well imperil the British position in Canada, particularly if the Canadian population were not conciliated. See A. L. Burt, *The Old Province of Quebec*, Toronto, 1933, pp. 154-55.

2. A. Shortt and A. G. Doughty, *Documents Relating to the Constitutional History of Canada 1759-1791*, Ottawa, 1918, I, p. 510: Memorial of the Foregoing French Petitioners in Support of their Petition.

3. *Ibid.*, p. 511.

4. The population of Canada according to the census of 1784 was 113,012 in the three districts of Quebec, Trois Rivières and Montreal (*Statistics of Canada*, Ottawa, Vol. IV, p. 74.) According to Carleton's evidence before the British parliament during the debates on the Quebec Act, the number of Protestants was "about three hundred and sixty besides women and children, in the whole colony of Canada." W. P. M. Kennedy, *Documents of the Canadian Constitution 1759-1915*, Toronto, 1918, p. 104.

5. Shortt and Doughty, II, p. 583: Carleton to Dartmouth, 23 Sep. 1774.

6. *Ibid.*, II, p. 585: Dartmouth to Carleton, 10 Dec. 1774.

7. According to Francis Masères giving evidence before the British parliament during the debates on the Quebec Act, the proportion of the trade in the hands of the English merchants was "seven-eights." He added, "The increase of the trade is an undoubted certainty. I am inclined to think it is entirely owing to the industry of the English merchants." (Kennedy, p. 114.)

8. Shortt and Doughty, I, pp. 295-96: Carleton to Shelburne, 20 Jan. 1768.

9. *Ibid.*, II, p. 587: Carleton to Dartmouth, 11 Nov. 1774.

10. Cf. *supra*, note 4.

11. Shortt and Doughty, II, p. 663: Dartmouth to Carleton 7 Jun. 1775.

12. *Ibid.*, II, p. 583: Gage to Carleton, 4 Sep. 1774.

13. *Ibid.*, II, p. 584: Carleton to Gage, 20 Sep. 1774.

14. Carleton to Gage, 4 Feb. 1775: quoted in R. Coupland, *The Quebec Act — A Study in Statesmanship*, Oxford, 1925, p. 141.

15. Quoted in R. Hargreaves, *The Bloodybacks*, London, 1968, p. 171.

16. Quoted in J. H. Smith, *Our Struggle for the Fourteenth Colony*, New York, 1907, 1, p. 79.

17. Quoted in J. C. Miller, *Origins of the American Revolution*, Boston, 1943, p. 374.

18. M. Farrand, *The Development of the United States*, London, 1919, p. 38.

19. Smith, I, p. 88.

20. Kennedy, pp. 139-43. For the French version of the Congress letter of 26 Oct. 1774, see Abbé Verreau, *Invasion du Canada, Collection de Mémoires recueillis et annotés*, Montréal, 1873, pp. 4-18.

21. Badeaux, p. 164. The Badeaux journal is included in the Verreau *Collection*.

22. Smith, I, p. 91. See facsimile letter.

23. *Ibid.*, p. 104.

24. Quoted in F. F. Van de Water, *Lake Champlain and Lake George*, New York, 1946, p. 154.

25. *The Narrative of Colonel Ethan Allen*, Corinth, New York, 1961, p. 5.

26. *Ibid.*, p. 10.

27. Smith, I, p. 139.

28. Allen, p. 9.

29. Smith, I, p. 156.

30. *A History of the Organization, Development and Services of the Military and Naval Forces of Canada*, Ottawa, n.d., III, p. 47: Allen to the Merchants of Montreal, 18 May 1775. This collection of documents was prepared by the Historical Section of the General Staff under the direction of Brigadier General Ernest Cruikshank. Further references will be indicated under his name.

31. Verreau, p. 33. The journal of Simon Sanguinet, in the Verreau collection, is entitled, *Témoin Oculaire de l'Invasion du Canada par les Bastonnois*.

32. Cruikshank, p. 47: Lettre adressée aux Habitants opprimés de la province de Québec, 29 May 1775, signed by John Hancock.

33. Miller, pp. 458-59.

34. Shortt and Doughty, II, p. 665: Carleton to Dartmouth, 7 Jan. 1775.

35. Sanguinet, p. 37.

36. Cruikshank, pp. 53-54: Proclamation 9 Jun. 1775.

37. *Ibid.*, p. 58: Carleton to Dartmouth, 26 Jun. 1775.

38. Sanguinet, p. 37.

39. Cruikshank, p. 61: Extract of a letter from Quebec, 20 Jul. 1775.

40. Francis Masères, *Additional Papers Concerning the Province of Quebec*, London, 1776, p. 101.

41. Cruikshank, p. 96: Extracts from the Records of Indian Transactions under the Superintendency of Guy Johnson, 1775.

42. *Ibid.*

43. Public Archives of Canada, Claus Papers, I, p. 209: Minutes of the Rebel Invasion of Canada, 1775. This document was published in 1906 by the Literary and Historical Society of Quebec, in *Blockade of Quebec in 1775-1776 by the American Revolutionists*.

44. Smith, I, pp. 301-302.

45. *New York Colonial Documents*, VIII, p. 660: Journal of Guy Johnson from May to November 1775.

46. K. C. Eyre, "Fort St. Jean 1666-1952," (unpublished honours thesis, Royal Military College of Canada, 1965), p. 46.

47. Cruikshank, pp. 101-102: Graves to Howe, 12 Oct. 1775.

II. The Montreal Campaign 1775

1. Lorimier gives the number as 72 Quebec Indians and 25 others. (See Lorimier's journal "Mes Services pendant la guerre Americaine" in Verreau, p. 248). Thomas Ainslie says there were 83 Indians. See S. Cohen, *Canada Preserved, the Journal of Captain Thomas Ainslie*, New York, 1968, p. 20.

2. Schuyler, in his letter to Washington, 20 Sep. 1775, does not specifically mention Hazen's name; but Smith I, p. 612, note XIX, is convinced that Hazen was the man who spoke to Schuyler and cites good evidence.

3. Quoted in Smith, I, p. 332.

4. W. M. Willett, *A Narrative of the Military Actions of Colonel Marinus Willett*, New York, 1831, p. 36.

5. Hazen was suspected of being a traitor but was not yet completely discredited. See Sanguinet, p. 65, and Lorimier, p. 251.

6. Cruikshank, p. 78: Livingston to the Captains of Militia, 16 Sep. 1775; and Livingston to Captains of Militia, 18 Sep. 1775.

7. Verreau, p. 165: Journal de J. B. Badeaux.

8. Sanguinet, p. 45. See also Cruikshank, p. 104: Tryon to Dartmouth, 11 Nov. 1775. The name appears in various sources as Oriet, Orillat and Orillac. In Tanguay the name appears as Aurillac.

9. Quoted in Van de Water, p. 174.

10. Allen, *Narrative*, p. 16.

11. Cruikshank, p. 79: Carleton to Dartmouth, 21 Sep. 1775.

12. Ainslie, p. 20.

13. Verreau, pp. 315-16: La Naudière to Baby, 28 Sep. 1775.

14. According to Allen's *Narrative*, p. 24, Prescott said to him, "I will not execute you now, but you shall grace a halter at Tyburn, God Damn ye."

15. Cruikshank, p. 7.

16. *Canadian Archives Report 1888*, pp. 892-93.

17. Cruikshank, p. 112: Carleton to Dartmouth, 25 Oct. 1775.

18. *Report of the Public Archives for 1914 and 1915*, Ottawa, 1916, Appendix B, p. 7: Prescott to Preston, 15 Sep. 1775.

19. *Ibid.*, p. 20: Preston Journal, 22 and 23 Sep. 1775.

20. *Ibid.*, p. 21: Preston Journal, 8 Oct. 1775.

21. *Ibid.*, p. 21: 6 Oct. 1775.

22. *Ibid.*, p. 23: 15 Oct. 1775.

23. *Ibid.*, p. 11: Hunter to Preston, 14 Oct. 1775.

24. *Ibid.*, p. 12: Hunter to Preston 17 Oct. 1775.

25. Smith, I, p. 426.

26. On 6 Oct. 1775, H. B. Livingston reported the American force as comprising 1000 in the main camp, 900 on the north side and 200 Canadians on the other side of the river (*American Magazine of History*, 1889, p. 256).

27. Verreau, p. 230. The journal of Berthelot d'Artigny is included in the Verreau collection. Berthelot says Maclean had 350 militia when he reached Trois Rivières and received more at that point. Some of these militiamen who joined Maclean at Sorel did so only to obtain muskets and then deserted.

28. Claus memorandum, p. 109. Claus stated that Montgomery had sent the Caughnawaga a substantial bribe of $1000 to remain neutral. Smith, I, p. 359, mentions the sum of £400.

29. Berthelot, p. 231. See also Lorimier, pp. 260-61, and Sanguinet, p. 66. Berthelot believed Carleton should have gone to Sorel and combined his forces with those of Maclean.

30. *Report of the Public Archives for 1914 and 1915*, pp. 12-13: Montgomery to Preston, 1 Nov. 1775.

31. *Ibid.*, p. 15: Montgomery to Preston, 2 Nov. 1775.

32. *Ibid.*, p. 16: Draft Articles of Capitulation.

33. *Ibid.*, p. 25: Preston Journal, 3 Nov. 1775.

34. Cruikshank, pp. 116-17: Carleton to Dartmouth, 5 Nov. 1775.

35. Quoted in Smith, I, p. 482.

36. Their letter to Montgomery is to be found in Sanguinet, p. 85.

37. Kenneth Roberts, *March to Quebec, Journals of the Members of Arnold's Expedition,* New York, 1938, p. 101: Arnold to Washington, 5 Dec. 1775.

38. Smith, I, p. 487.

39. *Journal of Charles Carroll of Carrolltown during his visit to Canada in 1776 as one of the Commissioners from Congress*, with a memoir and notes by Brantz Mayer, Maryland Historical Society, Baltimore, 1876, p. 97.

40. There are certain discrepancies in the several stories of Carleton's escape. I have followed the versions given by Berthelot in his Journal (p. 233-34), and by J. B. Badeaux, (pp. 176-77).

41. Quoted in P. E. Leroy, "Sir Guy Carleton as a Military Leader during the American Invasion and Repulse in Canada 1775-1776," (Ph.D. Thesis, Ohio State University, 1960) p. 105.

42. Ainslie, p. 22.

43. Cruikshank, p. 134: Carleton to Dartmouth, 20 Nov. 1775.

III. The Quebec Campaign 1775-1776

1. Henry, p. 301. The various journals quoted in this chapter are to be found in Roberts' *March to Quebec*. In each instance the page reference is to Roberts.

2. Smith, I, p. 525.

3. Senter, p. 203.

4. Thayer, p. 253.

5. Senter, p. 205.

6. Roberts, pp. 71-72: Arnold to Washington, 13 Oct. 1775.

7. *Ibid.*, pp. 70-71: Arnold to Schuyler, 13 Oct. 1775.

8. Cruikshank, pp. 99-100: Arnold to Mercier, 13 Oct. 1775.

9. Arnold, p. 55.

10. Senter, p. 210.

11. Thayer, p. 257.

12. Dearborn, p. 137.

13. Henry, p. 342.

14. Senter, p. 213.

15. Henry, p. 354.

16. *Ibid.*

17. *Ibid.*, p. 359.

18. Roberts, p. 90: Arnold to Montgomery, 29 Nov. 1775.

19. Henry, p. 360.

20. *The Quebec Gazette*, 6 Jul. 1775.

21. Ainslie, *op. cit.*, p. 19.

22. Cruikshank, p. 77: Proclamation, 16 Sep. 1775.

23. Ainslie, pp. 20-21.

24. Cruikshank, p. 120: Cramahé to Dartmouth, 9 Nov. 1775.

25. Cruikshank, p. 123, extract of a letter from Quebec, 9 Nov. 1775.

26. Quoted in Smith, II, p. 16.

27. *Ibid.*, II, p. 22.

28. Cruikshank, p. 130: Return of men for the defence, 16 Nov. 1775.

29. *Ibid.*, p. 131: Hamilton to Dartmouth, 20 Nov. 1775.

30. *Ibid.*, pp. 134-35: Proclamation, 22 Nov. 1775.

31. *Ibid.*, p. 168: Caldwell to Murray, 15 Jun. 1776.

32. Quoted in A. G. Bradley, *Lord Dorchester*, Toronto, 1907, pp. 118-19.

33. Ainslie, p. 28.

34. *Ibid.*

35. Smith, II, p. 106.

36. Ainslie, p. 29.

37. Senter, p. 230.

38. "Journal of the Most Remarkable Occurances in Quebec since Arnold Appeared before the Town," *Literary and Historical Society of Quebec, Seventh Series of Historical Documents*, Quebec, 1905, p. 101; 29 Dec. 1775.

39. Stocking, pp. 561-62.

40. Cruikshank, p. 137: General Order, 15 Dec. 1775, signed by Fred Weisenfels, Bde. Major.

41. Stocking, p. 562.

42. Ainslie, pp. 30-31.

43. Bradley, *Dorchester*, pp. 121-22. See also John Codman, *Arnold's Expedition to Quebec*, N.Y. 1903, pp. 203-204.

44. This letter, written by Montgomery to R. Livingston is quoted in Lt. Col. T. B. Strange, "Historical Notes on the Defence of Quebec in 1775," published in the papers of *The Literary and Historical Society of Quebec*, 1876, p. 38. See also "Journal of the Siege and Blockade of Quebec by the American rebels in autumn 1775 and winter 1776." *The Literary and Historical Society of Quebec*, 1876, p. 7. This is usually referred to as the Finlay Journal.

45. Ainslie, p. 31.

46. *Ibid.*, p. 33.

47. The account of the assault as given here is drawn from the several British diaries kept during the siege by Ainslie, Finlay and an anonymous artillery officer, the accounts written by Sanguinet and Caldwell, and the American diaries found in Roberts, *March to Quebec*.

48. Sanguinet, p. 118.

49. Dearborn, p. 149.

50. Henry, p. 377.

51. "Journal of the Siege from 1st Dec. 1775," *The Literary and Historical Society of Quebec*, 1906, p. 19. This journal is usually referred to as "The Journal of an Artillery officer," because the writer's duties seemed to be chiefly in the Batteries and on the Ramparts.

52. Finlay, p. 10.

53. Henry, p. 379.

54. Cruikshank, p. 138: Wooster to Warner, 6 Jan. 1776.

55. Cruikshank, pp. 140-41: Carleton to Howe, 12 Jan. 1776.

56. Roberts, p. 105: Arnold to Wooster, 2 Jan. 1776.

57. G. Lanctot, *Le Canada et la Révolution Américaine*, Montreal, 1965.

58. Quoted in Codman, pp. 267-68.

59. Ainslie, pp. 88-89.

60. Cruikshank, p. 162: Maclean, letter, 25 May 1776.

IV. Canada Liberated 1776

1. Smith, II, p. 218.
2. J. J. Lefebvre, *Les Canadiens Français et la Révolution*, Boston, 1949, pp. 10, 14.
3. Sanguinet, p. 89.
4. *Ibid.*, p. 93-4.
5. Quoted in Smith, II, p. 214. It should be noted, however, that several priests did support the Americans, including R. P. Floquet, who served as a chaplain in Hazen's regiment, and the Abbé Louis de Lotbinière, who served in the same capacity under Arnold at Quebec. See Lanctot, p. 138.
6. *Ibid.*, II, p. 235.
7. Badeaux, p. 196.
8. *The Quebec Gazette*, 5 Oct. 1775.
9. Sanguinet, pp. 103-105.
10. Quoted in Smith, II, p. 337.
11. This account is taken largely from *The Journal of Charles Carroll of Carrolltown during his visit to Canada in 1776, as one of the Commissioners from Congress*, with a memoir and notes by Brantz Mayer, Maryland Historical Society, Baltimore, 1876.
12. *Ibid.*, p. 93.
13. *Ibid.*, p. 32.
14. *Ibid.*, pp. 38-41. See also William Duane, *Canada and the Continental Congress*, Philadelphia, 1850, pp. 16-17.
15. Sanguinet, p. 81.
16. Quoted in D. Creighton, *The Empire of the St. Lawrence*, Toronto, 1956, p. 65.
17. *Ibid.*, p. 66.
18. Cruikshank, p. 27.
19. *An Authentic Narrative of Facts Relating to the Exchange of Prisoners taken at the Cedars: supported by the Testimony and depositions of His Majesty's Officers, with several Original Letters and Papers. Together With Remarks upon the Report and resolves of the American Congress on that subject*, London, 1777, p. 22.
20. *Ibid.*, p. 25.
21. *Ibid.*, p. 26.
22. Montigny and Capt. Lefebvre of the Vaudreuil Militia both claimed that they had captured Sherburn. But the American said that he surrendered to Lorimier. See Lorimier, p. 278.
23. *Authentic Account*, p. 29.
24. Lorimier, p. 281.
25. Quoted in C. H. Jones, *Campaign for the Conquest of Canada*, Philadelphia, 1882, p. 63.
26. James Wilkinson, *Memoirs of My Own Times*, Philadelphia, 1816, I, p. 47.
27. Included as appendix in *Authentic Account*. See also Berthelot, p. 237.
28. Cruikshank, p. 154.
29. Cruikshank, p. 155: Proclamation, 10 May 1776.
30. Quoted in North Callahan, *Daniel Morgan*, New York, 1961, p. 115.
31. Cruikshank, p. 152: Maclean to "My Lord," 10 May 1776.
32. Captain Thomas Pringle, R.N.
33. Quoted in Cruikshank, p. 30.
34. Fraser, Nesbitt and Lieutenant Colonel Patrick Gordon of the 28th were promoted to be brigadier generals on 9 Jun. 1777.
35. Badeaux, p. 218.
36. Berthelot, p. 238.

37. Cruikshank, pp. 174-75: Carleton to Germain, 20 Jun. 1776.

38. Smith, II, p. 416.

39. G. F. G. Stanley, *For Want of a Horse, being a Journal of the Campaigns against the Americans in 1776 and 1777 conducted from Canada, by an officer who served with Lt. Gen. Burgoyne*, Sackville, 1961, p. 71.

40. Berthelot, p. 240. Sanguinet, p. 134.

41. *For Want of a Horse*, p. 72.

42. Jones, p. 80.

43. Quoted in *ibid.*, p. 81-82.

44. Wilkinson, I, p. 51.

45. *Ibid.*, I, p. 55.

46. *Ibid.*, I, p. 58.

47. *For Want of a Horse*, p. 75: 18 Jun. 1776.

48. Wilkinson, I, p. 55.

49. John Fortescue, *History of the British Army 1763-1793*, London, 1911, III, p. 181.

50. Senter, p. 241.

51. Quoted in Smith, II, p. 450. The estimated loss sustained by the Americans in the Canadian invasion from killed, wounded, prisoners and died of sickness was 5000 men.

52. Cruikshank, p. 179: Carleton to Germain, 8 Jul. 1776.

53. *Ibid.*, p. 190: Carleton to Germain, 28 Sep. 1776.

54. *Ibid.*, p. 191: Carleton to Germain, 28 Sep. 1776.

55. *Ibid.*, p. 179: Carleton to Germain, 8 Jul. 1776.

56. *For Want of a Horse*, pp. 79-80: 26 Jul. 1776.

57. Wilkinson, I, p. 69.

58. E. T. Atkinson, "Some Evidence for Burgoyne's Expedition," *Journal of the Society for Army Historical Research*, Winter, 1948, pp. 132-42: Phillips to Fraser, 10 Sep. 1776.

59. Quoted in Jones, p. 99.

60. *For Want of a Horse*, p. 88: 12 Sep. 1776.

61. Quoted in Jones, p. 151.

62. James Hadden, *Journal and Orderly Books. A Journal kept in Canada and Upon Burgoyne's Campaign in 1776 and 1777*, Albany, 1884, p. 181.

63. It is hard to understand why the Americans consider the naval battle of Valcour Island one of the decisive battles of American history, unless it is because Pringle failed to secure the kind of victory his armament might have justified. What was decisive was that the removal of all Carleton's boats during the retreat and the construction of Arnold's fleet prevented Carleton from recovering Ticonderoga in 1776. See E. P. Hamilton, *Fort Ticonderoga, Key to a Continent*, Boston, 1964, pp. 161-62.

64. *For Want of a Horse*, p. 90: 19 Oct. 1776.

65. *Ibid.*, p. 90.

V. Rumours of War 1777-1779

1. Sanguinet, pp. 150-53.

2. Smith, II, p. 498.

3. *Ibid.*, II, p. 549.

4. Lanctot, pp. 202-203: Sanguinet, p. 153.

Index

A

B

D

I

Ile aux Grues, 107, 151.
Ile aux Noix, 39, 40, 41, 48, 132, 144, 145, 147.
Ile Dupas, 109.
Ile La Motte, 135, 137, 141.
Indians, Gage suggests employment of, 10, 23; British and Americans negotiate with, 31-34; at St. Jean, 39, 41; reluctant to attack Americans at Laprairie, 46; at capture of Allen, 46; some join Carleton, 48; in Carleton's relief force, 58-59; assemble at Oswegatchie, 117; attack Americans at the Cedars, 119-21; plunder Americans at the Cedars, 120; Indians and the cartel, 121-23; pursue retreating Americans, 132; patrol Canadian frontier, 136; at Valcour Island, 142.
Indian nations
  Caughnawaga, 26, 31, 33, 34, 58, 118.
  Cayuga, 117.
  Conosadaga, 59, 123.
  Mississauga, 117.
  Mohawk, 32, 34.
  Oneida, 32.
  Onondaga, 34.
  St. Regis, 34, 48, 119.
  Seneca, 117, 121.
  Seven Nations of Canada, 31, 33.
  Six Nations, 31.
  Stockbridge, 34, 136.
  Tuscarora, 32.
Indian territory, 4, 32.
Irvine, William, 128.

J

Jacques Cartier, 116, 126.
Jeune Lorette, 124.
Johnson, Guy, 32-34, *passim*; 117, 150.
Johnson, John, 134, 150.
Johnson, Peter, 34, 47.
Johnson, William, 12, 32.

K

Kalb, Baron de, 146.
Kamouraska, 124, 144.
Kaskaskia, 32.

L

Lachenaie, 30.
Lachine, 29, 33, 121, 123.
La Corne, Saint Luc de, 59.
Lacoste, Monsieur, 59, 60, 61.

T

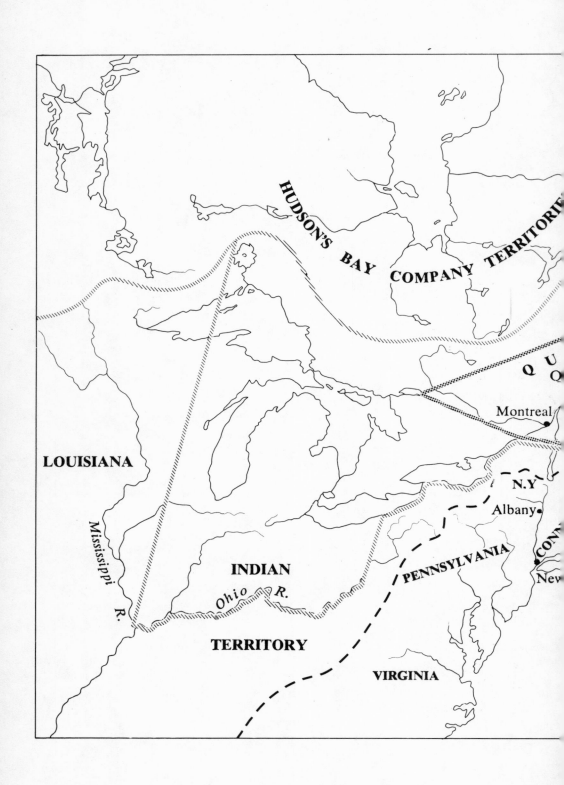

HUDSON'S BAY COMPANY TERRITORIES

QU
Q

Montreal

LOUISIANA

N.Y

Albany

Mississippi R.

INDIAN

Ohio R.

PENNSYLVANIA

CON

New

TERRITORY

VIRGINIA